A JOKEBOOK
FOR ALL REASONS

—lampoon your favorite lawyer
—shrink the finest psychiatrist
—addle your in-laws
—best your boss
—amuse any audience

With this convenient, comprehensive sourcebook of incomparable American humor, you'll never be at a loss for words.

1,001
GREAT JOKES

1,001 GREAT JOKES

JEFF ROVIN

A SIGNET BOOK

NEW AMERICAN LIBRARY

NAL BOOKS ARE AVAILABLE AT QUANTITY DISCOUNTS WHEN USED
TO PROMOTE PRODUCTS OR SERVICES. FOR INFORMATION PLEASE
WRITE TO PREMIUM MARKETING DIVISION, NEW AMERICAN
LIBRARY, 1633 BROADWAY, NEW YORK, NEW YORK 10019.

SIGNET TRADEMARK REG. U.S. PAT. OFF. AND FOREIGN COUNTRIES
REGISTERED TRADEMARK—MARCA REGISTRADA
HECHO EN CHICAGO, U.S.A.

SIGNET, SIGNET CLASSIC, MENTOR, ONYX, PLUME,
MERIDIAN and NAL BOOKS are published by NAL PENGUIN INC.,
1633 Broadway, New York, New York 10019

First Printing, April, 1987

        4   5   6   7   8   9

PRINTED IN THE UNITED STATES OF AMERICA

INTRODUCTION

Everyone loves to laugh. (Well . . . almost everyone, but more on that in a bit.) Kings beheaded their wives but kept their court jesters, and who remembers very much of what Gerald Ford did except slide down steps and crown people with golf balls. (Some pundits include the Nixon pardon among Mr. Ford's jokes, but that's another story.) Woodrow Wilson was arguably a better president than John Kennedy, but volumes of Wilson Wit are scarce and we remember him less fondly.

Sitcoms are perennially the most popular shows on TV, Johnny Carson and Bob Hope endure while "serious" performers like James Caan and Al Pacino are box office death, and on the concert stage Joan Rivers and David Brenner still draw sold-out houses while the likes of Boy George can't get himself arrested. (At least, not for singing.)

The New York *Herald Tribune* is gone but *Mad* is still here, no one but the writer's mother turns to the latest prose in *Playboy* or *The New Yorker* before they've had a look at the cartoons, and who among us wouldn't swap the Sunday *Times'* tedious Week in Review for a good (or even passable) collection of funnies?

Producers who give the public a good comedy like *Ghostbusters*, *Tootsie*, or *Beverly Hills Cop*, or even a lame comedy like *Spies Like Us*, usually make a fortune. Even in his greatest tragedies Shakespeare took time out from the bloodletting to make us laugh; not so Milton and Thomas Mann, who are read less and enjoyed largely by those who turn to Vonnegut in *Playboy* even before they crack the centerfold. By and large, people find Mozart's *The Magic Flute* infinitely more entertaining than Moussorgsky's *Boris Godounoff* because of Mozart's levity. (Surely Moussorgsky could have given the clerk Tchelkaloff a few good lines or a clever aria. "Who's Czarry Now?" might have been appropriate.)

And, of course, joke books sell well, too.

But greed only *partly* explains why we've put this book together. Despite the many joke compendia on the market, very, very few allow you to find gags on specific topics unless you're looking for something "truly tasteless" or "totally gross," in which case it's a cinch. This book fills that void by gathering jokes according to *subject*. Thus, whether you're a vivisectionist who wants a gag about mice to break the tension during your next skin graft, or a Texan tour guide looking for a joke about the Alamo, you'll find it quickly among the over one thousand jokes catalogued and cross-referenced in this book.

(Incidentally, there are also a couple of off-color jokes herein, a few that the other volumes missed or some that are simply gems. We included these largely to make a First Amendment stand against the recent Meese Commission attack on pornography. The possibility of selling a few extra copies played no part in our decision.)

Needless to say, in order to present the finest jokes ever written or uttered, we pored over countless sources, many of them going as far back as Milton. None was written by Jocular John (though he did *allude* to "Laughter holding both his sides" in *Lycidas*, proving that he might have become a wittier writer had he not been soured by blindness and arrest after supporting the losing side in the English Civil War). However, we *did* spend many hours tracking down the original manuscript of Coleridge's *The Rime of the Ancient Mariner*. Alas, there's no truth to the rumor that the author began his unexpurgated poem, "It is an Ancient Mariner,/And he stoppeth one of three./And asked the long grey bearded man, 'Hear ye the one about the albatross who had one wing shorter than the other and flew up his own bung?' "

Getting serious for a moment:

Only one in thirty jokes collected for this opus made their way into the finished dictionary. Many were variations on existing jokes, and many more simply weren't funny. Humor may well be subjective, but if Mr. Meese *really* wants to persecute the press he ought to hunt down the authors of Edsels like, "Ever hear of lilac time? It's 3:00 A.M. You come walking in, your wife asks where you've been, and you lilac hell." We could publish an *encyclopedia* for comedic misfires; not only doesn't a lot of humor date well, but so much of it isn't universal. What gets laughs in the Borscht Belt often doesn't play in Peoria. And it was important that in addition to being a *complete* book of great humor, we also put together a *universal* book of great humor.

Which we believe this is. Yet in addition to being funny and eclectic, *1,001 Great Jokes* also aspires to be the most *functional* joke book ever compiled. Speakers, students looking to spice up a research paper, radio and TV emcees (especially the humorless Donahue), politicians, the clergy, and even the casual reader will all find useful and entertaining material herein. Business people will find the book particularly useful. We've all heard of Power Lunching and Dressing for Success. Well, don't discard the notion of punning your way to the top. Ever hear Lee Iacocca speak? He's a lot funnier than Frank Borman ever was at Eastern; which man would *you* bet on in a race for the Presidency?

Speaking of people without a sense of humor— that humorless soul we mentioned earlier—he was none other than that old sourpuss, the Earl of Chesterfield, and he once huffed, "In my mind, there is nothing so illiberal and so ill-bred as audible laughter." However, it was also the earl who had the audacity to try to become a sponsor of Samuel Johnson's classic *Dictionary of the English Language*—*after* that volume had already been finished. Johnson's rebuke is legendary and acid with humor: he thanked the earl for being one who "looks with unconcern on a Man struggling in the water and when he has reached ground encumbers him with help."

So read this book and laugh aloud, for as the wise Ella Wheeler Wilcox more accurately put it, "Laugh and the world laughs with you."

1. A think tank researching the ability of humans to survive under extreme circumstances received a multinational grant to study what in a person's background increased or decreased his capacity to survive in the wild. Selecting an American, a Frenchman, and a Japanese for the program, the researchers assigned them specific tasks. The American was put in charge of shelter, the Frenchman in charge of food, and the Japanese in charge of supplies.

Flying the men to a desert island, the researchers left them there for six months.

Returning to the island, the group was surprised to find a beautiful house on the beach. Entering, they were greeted by the American who showed them around. They were impressed with what he'd done: the floors were snuggly fitted planks, the walls coated with homemade paint, and the thatched roof leakproof. Venturing into the kitchen, they were welcomed by the Frenchman, who showed them a larder stocked with meats, vegetables, fish, coconut milk, fruits, and other comestibles. Out back, he had erected a pen for keeping wild pigs he had caught, and he had grown a substantial garden.

"And tell me," said the leader of the research group, "where is our Japanese friend?"

"Well, sir," said the American, "the truth is, we haven't seen him since the day we landed."

Concerned, the scientists hastily formed a search party and ventured into the woods to find him. No sooner had they set out than the Oriental leaped from a tree and shouted. "Supplize!"

2. The bartender said to Mr. Jones, "Bet I can make you do an impression of a train."

Being a gambling man, Jones lay five bucks on the counter. "Try your best."

"Knock-knock."

"Who's there?"

"Chooch."

"Chooch who?"

The bartender smiled and pocketed the money. Angry at having been taken, Jones glanced at a black man sitting at the end of the bar. Moseying over, he said, "Hey . . . five bucks says I can make you do an impression of a train."

The black man shrugged and placed his money on the table.

"Knock-knock."

"Who's there?"

"Chooch."

"Who be Chooch?"

3. Q: What is fo-fi-fo, fo-fi-fi-fo?

   A: A black girl giving out her telephone number.

4. Newly arrived in Beverly Hills from Mississippi, Rufus got a job as a gardener. At the end of his first day on the job, he knocked on the door and his boss, Mr. Mayer, answered.

   "Missuh Mayuh, suh, you know where I kin find me sum hose?"

   Mayer shrugged. "We keep it in the garage, of course."

   "Ah," Rufus sighed, "thass Bev'ly Hills for yuh. In Mississippi, ah hadda go all the way to the streetco'nuh."

5. "A wrench," said the sage, "is where Jewish people go to ride horses."

6. Out to lunch one day, the immigrants were having a fine time until Hymie began to gag.

   "I—I tink I svallowed a bone," Hymie gasped.

   "Hymie," said Miklos, "are you choking?"

   "No, demmit, I'm serious!"

7. Then there was the young woman who taught English to immigrants at the turn of the century. Everyone was coming along well so she moved on to some complicated phrasing.

   "Now that you're in America," she told the class, "two words you'll be seeing a lot of are *commercial* and *official* in a sentence. Josef, do you think you could use those two words in a sentence?"

"Soitenly," replied the Austrian immigrant. "Come, Moishel, and eat a fishel."

8. Sitting at a counter in the local diner, a young woman was mortified when two immigrants sitting beside her began talking.

"Emma comma first," said one man, "then I comma, then the two asses they comma together, then I comma again, then the two asses more comma, then I comma again and pee-pee, then I comma for the last time."

Collaring the waitress as she passed, the young woman said, "How can you possibly allow such vile men to eat in this establishment?"

"Vile?" barked the waitress. "Honey, what's vile about spelling *Mississippi*?"

9. "So," said Sadie to her sister from the old country, "how do you like sex?"

"What," replied her sister, "de one on Fifth Avenue or de one in Yonkers?"

ACCOUNTANTS   *See also* BANKING, FINANCE
                             and THE OFFICE 4

1. The worst kind of accountant to have is the shy, retiring type. His ledgers are a few million dollars shy, which is why he's retiring.

2. That accountant was related to the one who figured out how to keep from spending a dime in eight years. He'll be out in a week.

3. Then there was the accountant who told his client, "There's good news, and there's bad news."

   "Give me the bad news first," the client said nervously.

   "The bad news is that your business is flat on its back."

   The businessperson asked hopefully, "And what's the good news?"

   "It's looking up."

4. "I don't understand," asked the ditzy accountant. "If you're selling these computers way under cost, how is it you're showing a profit?"

   "Simple," said the businessman. "We make our money fixing them."

5. However, the most successful accountant of all was the one who took his father's advice and carved a career for himself. He became a chiseler.

6. The accountant came to work looking more bedraggled than any of his coworkers had ever seen him. Finally his boss took him aside.

   "Barry," he said, "you look like hell. What's wrong?"

   "Sorry," he replied, "I just couldn't get to sleep last night."

Trying to be helpful, Barry's boss said, "Why didn't you try counting sheep?"

"I did," he answered, "and that was the problem. I made a mistake, and it took me the rest of the night to find it."

ADOPTION

1. The backwoods couple was delighted when finally their long wait to adopt a baby came to an end. The adoption center called and told them they had a wonderful Japanese boy, and the couple took him without hesitation.

On the way back home, they stopped by the local college to enroll in night courses.

After they filled out the form, the registration clerk inquired, "May I ask you a question? What ever possessed you to study Japanese?"

The backwoodsman said proudly, "In a year or so, our adopted son will start to talk. We want to be able to understand him."

ADVERTISING   *See also* DIETS 1

1. The youthful advertising executive had made a name for himself by getting athletes to use clothing or gear that bore a client's name. However, his greatest coup was convincing boxers to accept advertising on the bottoms of their shoes. . . .

1. Worried because they hadn't heard anything for days from the widow in the neighboring apartment, Mrs. Silver said to her son, "Timmy, would you go next door and see how old Mrs. Kirkland is?"

   A few minutes later, Timmy returned.

   "Well," asked Mrs. Silver, "is she all right?"

   "She's fine, except that she's pissed at you."

   "At me?" the woman exclaimed. "Whatever for?"

   "She said it's none of your business how old she is."

2. Runner Jim Simpson was the oldest man ever to compete in the Olympics. Granting an interview prior to the big match, the eighty-year-old told the reporter that he didn't consider himself extraordinary at all.

   "Heck," he said, "my dad's 102 and still runs a farm . . . and the only reason he ain't here is 'cause he's best man at the wedding of my 130-year-old grandad."

   "Amazing," said the reporter. "I can't imagine someone wanting to get married at that age."

   "*Want* nuthin'," said Simpson. "Grandad *has* to get married."

3. The census taker knocked on Mrs. May's door, and the old spinster was glad to answer all of his questions. However, when it came to the question of her age, she balked.

"But madam," the census taker assured her, "everyone tells me their age."

"Everyone?" she asked doubtfully.

"That's right."

"Even Daisy Hill down the street? And her sister Hilda next door?"

"They did."

"In that case," said Mrs. May, "put me down as the same age."

"As old as the Hills," the census taker wrote obligingly.

AIRPLANES   *See also* TRAVEL and PRESIDENTS 5

1. While cruising at nearly forty thousand feet, the airplane shuddered and Mr. Benson looked out the window.

"Good Lord!" he screamed, "one of the engines just blew up!"

Other passengers left their seats and came running over; suddenly the aircraft was rocked by a second blast as yet another engine exploded on the other side.

The passengers were in a panic now, and even the stewardesses couldn't maintain order. Just then, standing tall and smiling confidently, the pilot strode from the cockpit and assured everyone that there was nothing to worry about. His words and his demeanor seemed to assuage most of the passengers, who sat back down as the pilot calmly walked to the door of the aircraft. There, he grabbed several packages from under the seats and began handing them to the flight attendants. Each crew member attached the package to his back.

"Say," spoke up an alert passenger, "aren't those parachutes?"

The pilot said they were.

The passenger went on, "But I thought you said there was nothing to worry about?"

"There isn't," replied the pilot as a third engine exploded. "We're going to get help."

THE ALAMO

1. Davy Crockett climbed to the ramparts of the Alamo. Below, pacing not far from the main gate, was a Mexican sentry.

"Twenty, twenty, twenty," Crockett cried out. A few moments later he repeated the call. "Twenty, twenty, twenty."

This went on for most of the night, baffling the Mexican no end. There were only Mexicans outside the gate, none whom Crockett could possibly be signaling; finally his curiosity got the best of him.

"Hey, meester," said the Mexican. "You been calling 'Twenty, twenty, twenty' ever seence I came on duty. *Madre de Dios*, why?"

Crockett leaned on his rifle. "Y'wanna know why?" he asked.

"Yes, I do."

"Ya'll have to come up here with me."

"Fine . . . anything."

Crockett looked furtively around. "Okay. Come around back and tell the guard Davy sent ya; he'll let ya in."

Less than a minute later the Mexican was standing beside his enemy on the ramparts of the ramshackle mission.

"Well?" he demanded.

Crockett smiled and pointed into the fortress. "Look down here, just inside the front gate."

The Mexican did as he was told, bending over and peering down from the wall. The instant he did so, Crockett booted him in the seat, and he fell to his death. Looking across the prairie where the Mexican army was camped, Crockett leaned on his rifle and yelled, "Twenty-one, twenty-one, twenty-one. . . ."

AMERICAN REVOLUTION

1. Tearing from the stable on his historic midnight ride, Paul Revere pulled up in front of the first house on the street.

"Hello!" he yelled up, "is the man of the house at home!"

"I am," came the groggy reply.

"Then arm yourself, for the British approach!"

Revere rode on and repeated his message at the next six stops. At the eighth house he called again, and a woman came to the window.

"Is your husband at home!" he cried. "The British are coming!"

"I'm sorry," she said, "but he's in Paris on business."

"Whoa!"

ANATOMY   *See also* CLERGY 5

1. "Ms. Perkins," said the biology teacher, his eyes pinning the daydreaming student, "would you please tell the class which portion of the human anatomy swells to ten times its normal size during periods of agitation or emotional excitement?"

Blushing, the woman stammered, "Professor, I—I would r-rather n-not answer that q-question."

Arching a brow, the professor asked, "Oh? And why not?"

"W-well, s-sir, that's kind of . . . p-personal."

"Not at all," he blustered. "The correct answer is the pupil of the eye, and your response tells me two things: First, that you didn't read last night's assignment, and second, that marriage is going to leave you a tremendously disappointed young woman."

2. Depressed about the size of his manhood, the plastic surgeon decided to hang himself.

ANIMALS   *See also* CATS, DOGS, ELEPHANTS, HORSES, INSECTS, PETS, TAXIDERMY, WORMS, ZOOS, and BABIES 8, THE CIRCUS 6, 7, CLOTHING 3, THE ENVIRONMENT 5, FARMERS 2, 4, 5, FLATULENCE 8, HUNTERS 3, LAWYERS 7, MORONS 15, NATIVES 3, POLICE 4, PSYCHIATRISTS 2, TRAVEL 8, TRUCKERS 1

1. A woman woke up one morning to find a ferocious-looking gorilla in a tree on her African plantation. She quickly phoned the local game warden, who arrived minutes later. In one hand he held a shotgun, and in the other the leash of a fierce Doberman pinscher.

As they walked to the tree, the warden explained, "What's going to happen is that I go up the tree, throw the gorilla out, and the dog clamps his teeth on the gorilla's balls."

The woman nodded and was surprised when he handed her the gun.

"You know how to use this?" he asked.

"I do," she said, "but what's it for?"

The warden replied, "Well . . . sometimes the gorillas are pretty tough and throw *me* out of the tree. If that happens, I want you to do one thing."

"Shoot the gorilla?"

"No," he answered, "the dog."

2. The bear had to move his bowels and lumbered into the woods. As chance would have it, he found a rabbit doing the same. Squatting beside the hare, the bear asked, "Say, do you have trouble with shit sticking to your fur?"

The rabbit finished up and shook his head. "None whatsoever."

Nodding, the bear completed his own chore. "That's good," he growled and, grabbing the bunny, used him to wipe his ass.

3. Two mice are making their way through a whorehouse when one of them stops to admire a woman's naked bottom.

"Nice, huh?"

"So-so," says the other. "Me? I'm a titmouse."

4. Q: What did the giraffe say when he swaggered into the bar?

A: "The highballs are on me."

5. Then there was the snake who got horny while she was out with her date. She stopped and he crawled on.

6. Mary walked into the pet store and, after looking up and down the aisles, asked the proprietor for help.

"I'd like a box of birdseed," said the lady.

"For which kind of bird?" he asked helpfully.

"Oh, I dunno," the strange woman replied. "Whichever will grow the fastest."

7. Q: Why do mice have small balls?
A: Because so few know how to dance.

8. Then there was the stork who complained that he had a bad reputation for finishing the job that began with a lark. . . .

9. Q: What did the Indian say when he'd bagged a doe without eyes?
A: I have no eye deer.

9. Luigi the organ grinder wasn't doing much business in the middle of the street, so he decided to move down to the corner, near the bus stop. There he cranked his music box, smiling broadly for passersby, as the monkey flit about trying to stir up business.

On one particularly busy day, Luigi was so busy watching the parade of new faces that he failed to pay much attention to the monkey. Unbeknownst to him, the plucky little ape approached a young man waiting for the bus, scurried up his leg and onto his jacket, and promptly poked his penis in the man's ear. He proceeded to hump away, his little monkey claws holding tightly so the man couldn't dislodge him.

"Hey!" shouted the man, turning to the organ grinder, "do you know your monkey's screwing my goddam ear!"

"No," said the organ grinder solicitously, "but if you'll hum a few bars. . . ."

10. The two goats of German extraction wandered from the farm and, before long, they found themselves in a junkyard. There they spotted an abandoned car and began dining.

When the goats didn't return that night, the farmer went out looking for them. After hours of following their little goat tracks, he found the two bloated animals sleeping off their big meal.

"What the hell have you two been up to?" he shook them awake.

"Vhy . . . ve vent for a valk."

"Yes," said the other, "and ve found a nice car to eat."

"A car?" yelled the farmer. "What kind of car?"

Thinking back, one of the goats said, "It vas a Ford V-8."

11. The sailor's parrot was a splendid companion except for one thing: He was constantly horny and always complaining about it. Home from a long voyage, the sailor decided to go to church

and ask the priest whether it was ethical to frustrate the bird like that.

Much to the sailor's surprise, the priest said, "My son, it just so happens that I too have a parrot at home. Unlike yours, however, my Penelope sits in her cage and prays devoutly day in and day out. Perhaps if we were to put them together, her godliness might rub off on your bird."

Agreeing that it was worth a try, the sailor went to the pastor's house that night, and after the birds were placed in the same cage, the two men retired to give them their privacy.

Having been briefed by his owner, the cocky parrot spit from the side of its mouth and circled the smaller Penelope. "So," he sneered, "you're gonna reform me, huh?"

"Not at all," she cooed, stepping over and eyeing him seductively. "What the hell do you think I've been praying for all these years?"

12. The eternal porpoises lived in a landlocked lake along the Ivory Coast of Africa. At one time the lake had been connected to the Gulf of Guinea; now the only way they could feed on the baby sea gulls that enabled them to live forever was if the natives of the Ngubi tribe captured them in the gulf and brought them to the lake.

The natives performed this sacred duty for centuries but lately lions had taken to hunting the valley that led from the Ngubi lands to the shore. Thus it became necessary for the natives to spend a great deal of time distilling and manufacturing a sleeping potion which, with tremendous care, the bravest of the Ngubi warriors dispensed via poison dart before making their way through the valley.

Unfortunately, this process put an enormous drain on the treasury of the tribe. Not only was the poison costly to make, but the time the warriors spent putting the lions to sleep should have been used for hunting. Thus, the chief was forced to put a new law on the Ngubi books: He made it illegal to transport young gulls across sedate lions for immortal porpoises.

ANTIQUES

1. Upon arriving home with their new purchase, the couple set up a clock that had belonged to the late President Truman. After tinkering with it for a while, the wife sat back and looked despondently at her husband.

   "It may be beautiful," she said, "but now I know why he was late."

2. According to statistics, last year over 17 million American families paid a lot of money for things that looked funny and didn't work. Seven million of these were antiques; the rest were college students.

1. The archaeologist was thrilled beyond words when, after digging in Australia, he found a tablet with symbols carved upon it. Carbon dating placed it at nearly two thousand years old, which made the find even more significant.

"If we look at these symbols," said the archaeologist at a press conference, "we can infer several things about the society that carved them." Displaying the tablet, he pointed out the symbols in turn. "The presence of the cross," said he, "indicates that Christianity had reached Australia not long after its founding. Next, the presence of a shovel suggests that the early Australians were builders. The third symbol, what looks to be a donkey, proves that they had domesticated animals, while the fourth picture, a baby fowl, demonstrates that they were farmers."

"Bull!" shouted a man in the audience, an archaeologist noted for his outré ideas. "Anyone with half a brain knows that it's really early Australian pornography."

"Oh?" the discoverer of the tablets said smugly, "and how do you know that?"

"Because," he replied, "what it *really* says is, 'Christ, dig the ass on that chick!' "

2. The three amateur archaeologists were exploring a temple deep in the jungles of the Amazon when they were captured by a tribe of hostile natives.

"You have profaned the ancient temple of our fertility goddess," exhorted the chief. "For that, you must surrender your manhood."

Approaching the first man, he asked, "What is your job in your native land?"

Puzzled the man said, "I—I'm a butcher, sir."

The chief ordered, "Then we shall chop it off!" Approaching the second man, he said, "What is your job in your native land?"

Drawing himself up proudly, he said, "I'm a fire fighter."

"Then we shall burn yours off," he said, and went on to the third man. "And what is your job in your native land?"

Having seen what was ordered for his friends, the man said confidently, "I'm a lumberjack, Your Lordship."

"Very well," he said. "For you, we shall jack it off!"

ARTISTS

1. The sculptor and one of his students went out for coffee after class.

"You have the most delicate, slender hands,"

said the student, a comely young lady. "Forgive me for saying it, but they belong on a woman."

Not only did he forgive her, he obliged.

AUTOMOBILES *See also* AUTOMOBILE ACCIDENTS and NUDISM 3

1. "The difference between a good car and a lemon is gunning," Tim said to Tony.

    Tony, who always thought he was *au courant* about automobiles, said, "I don't follow."

    "Well," said Tim, "with a good car, you gun the engine. With a lemon, you gun the salesperson."

2. Then there was the new car buyer who insisted on buying a car with a twelve-month warranty. He said the only thing he'd ever had last a full year on a car was aggravation.

3. "And I don't even have to worry about changing the oil every thousand miles," said the disgruntled owner of a grade A lemon. "There's never any left."

1. It was the first time Jeryl and Paul had gone out together, and the impatient girl was frustrated beyond words at how slowly Paul was driving.

"Listen," she said at last, "I'll make a deal with you. Each time you speed up another ten miles an hour, I'll take off an article of clothing."

Licking his lips, Paul put the pedal to the floor. At thirty miles an hour, she removed her blouse. At forty, off came her pants. At fifty, she slipped off her bra, and at sixty her panties. At that point, Paul's attention wasn't on the road, and he lost control of the car. The vehicle spun down an incline, turning over and over until it landed at the bottom, pinning all but Paul's legs beneath it.

Squirming out, Jeryl grabbed one of Paul's shoes, which was the only article of clothing she could reach and, holding it in front of her vagina, hurried back to the road. There she flagged down the first person who came along, a trucker.

"Sir," she said frantically, still trying to conceal herself with the shoe, "you've got to help me! My boyfriend is stuck!"

"Lady," whistled the truck driver, "if he's in that deep, there ain't nothin' I can do t' help him."

BABIES See also KIDS, TEST-TUBE BABIES, and CLOTHING 11, SCHOOL 10

1. After the birth of his daughter, Mr. Abram sat brooding in the waiting room. Noticing the gloomy father, the obstetrician went over to him.

"Excuse me, Bill, but why the long face?"

Mr. Abram looked up. "To tell the truth, doc, I didn't want a daughter." He balled his fist. "I was hoping for a kid who had—you know, a *penis*."

Trying to cheer him up, the doctor pat him on the shoulder and said, "Don't worry. In about eighteen years, she'll have a fine place to put one."

2. Making the rounds of the maternity ward, a visiting obstetrician pointed to a child who was smaller and more fragile than the rest.

"What's wrong with that one?" he asked the head nurse.

"Nothing, doctor," she replied. "He's a test-tube baby, and they tend to be smaller than others."

"It just goes to show," the obstetrician said sagely, "spare the rod and spoil the child."

3. Then there was the thick-skulled Mrs. Lytton who had to stop breastfeeding her infant son. It hurt too much when she boiled the nipples.

4. "My three-year-old's been walking since she was two," the mother told her ditzy friend Zelda.

"Gosh," said Zelda, "doesn't she ever get tired?"

5. Then there was Ralph, who had children for the deductions, only to discover, too late, how taxing they could be.

6. Laurel and Loren were an extremely liberal, though not especially bright, white couple. Wanting to begin a family, they decided they wanted to have a black baby, and set to work. Nine months later, the fruits of their labor was born: a lovely white girl. Pleased but disappointed, Loren decided to ask a black man at work why they hadn't parented a black baby.

Realizing that Loren was somewhat sluggish, the fellow took him aside and asked, "Is your penis at least a foot long?"

Loren had to admit that it was not.

"And is it at least four inches wide?"

Once more Loren replied in the negative.

"Well, man, there's your problem!" the chap slapped him on the back. "You let in too much light!"

7. Laurel and Loren finally had three children before they stopped. Liberal as they were, they knew that one in every four babies born is Chinese, and they only wanted American children.

8. Q: What's the difference between cows and infants?
A: Cows turn water into milk. . . .

BALDNESS

1. "Yes," said the balding man, "split hair *is* a problem. Mine split about five years ago."

BALLERINAS

1. Q: Why do ballerinas wear tights?
A: So they don't stick to the floor when they do splits.

1. Looking at her own scribbled stenography, one secretary leaned over to another who had been in the meeting. "I can't remember," she said. "Did Mr. Porter say you 'retire a loan.' "

   "Not if I can help it," the girl replied.

2. Standing in line at the bank, one businessperson said to another, "What really pisses me off about banking is that you give them your money freely, but when you try to borrow any they want to know if you're good for it!"

3. After reading the complicated instructions for the automatic teller, the confused customer walked over to a bank officer.

   "Excuse me," said the customer, "but I was wondering if you could help me out."

   "Certainly," smiled the officer. "Go right through that door."

BASEBALL   *See also* BOXING, FOOTBALL, GOLF,
              HOCKEY, SOCCER, WRESTLING, and BEER 1

1. Once there was the pitcher whose career as a
   ladies' man ended when he caught a line drive
   on the fly. . . .

2. Then there was the Tiger with four balls. He
   walked to first base.

3. The father was thrilled when his daughter called
   from college, though his mood changed drasti-
   cally when she told him that she'd made the
   softball team.

4. Which wasn't as bad as the moron who couldn't
   understand why a pitcher earning a half-million
   dollars a year needed relief.

BATHROOMS

1. "Mom," little Alexander asked, "does Jesus use
   our bathroom?"
       "Why, no!" his mother said sweetly. "Why do
   you ask?"

"Cause every morning, daddy kicks the door and yells, "Christ, are you still in there?"

2. Little Ashley and his friend Beaufort went to the movies and, before the show, headed to the bathroom to relieve themselves. Ashley urinated, then washed his hands; much to his surprise, Beaufort did just the opposite.

"Hey," said Ashley, "smart boys wash after they pee."

Holding his head back proudly, young Beaufort corrected, "Smart boys learn not to pee on their hands."

BEER   See also DRINKING and DEAFNESS 1,
                            SINGLES 5, SUPERHEROES 1

1. Milt Famie was the greatest pitcher the major leagues had ever seen. But beer was his fatal weakness, and when he drank before a game he couldn't hurl a strike to save his life.

Thanks to his pitching skills, Milt got his team into the World Series. But the pressure of the playoffs proved too much, and, with the score tied in the ninth inning of the seventh and deciding game, Milt snuck off and chugged down one too many brews. Returning to the mound, he walked the last four batters, and his team lost by a single run.

Cornered by the press after the game, the winning pitcher credited his opponent with having a lot of talent and heart, summing up the loss thusly: "It's the beer that made Milt Famie walk us!"

2. "Pour me a cold one," said the teenager walking into the bar.

Looking him over, the barmaid said, "Scat, kid, you want to get me in trouble?"

"Maybe later," he replied. "Right now all I want's a beer."

3. Then there was the brewery employee's widow who wasn't able to collect her husband's insurance when he drowned in a vat. Eyewitnesses swore he got out four times to piss.

4. The rope was walking down the street and, feeling a bit thirsty, popped into a bar.

"Excuse me," he said to the bartender in his high, rope voice, "but I'd like a beer."

The bartender looked at him oddly. "Say, are you . . . a rope?"

"Yes, sir, I am."

The man's features clouded. "Then get out! I'm not going to serve beer to a rope!"

Dejected, the rope left and spotted a second bar down the street. Ambling in, he sat himself on a stool and asked the bartender for a beer.

"Hold on," said the bartender, "aren't you—a rope?"

"Yes, but I can pay—"

"Forget it," snapped the bartender, "we don't cater to ropes in this establishment."

Mortified, the rope left. Noticing yet another bar down the road, the rope was determined not to be turned away again. Tangling himself up and vigorously rubbing both of his ends on the concrete, he boldly strode into the bar.

"Pardon me," he said to the bartender, "but I'd like a beer."

"Wait a minute," said the bartender, "aren't you a rope?"

"No," the rope replied, "I'm a frayed knot."

THE BIBLE   *See also* CLERGY, HEAVEN,
                          RELIGION, and BUSINESS 7,
                                         WORMS 1

1. Adam and Eve had finished having sex for the first time, and as Adam lay on the soft grasses of Eden, God appeared before him.

"Well, my son," said the Lord, "how didst thou like it?"

"Oh!" gushed Adam, "it was *incredible*! I can't *tell* you how much I enjoyed it."

"And what didst Eve think?"

"She liked it too," smiled Adam.

The Lord looked around. "Then tell me, Adam, where is thy mate?"

Gesturing toward the edge of the Garden, Adam said, "She's over by the river, Lord, washing."

Suddenly the skies darkened, and God tore at his hair in anguish.

"What is it?" cried Adam, cowering behind a tree trunk, "what's wrong?"

"Wrong?" boomed the Lord, "now I'll *never* get that smell out of the fish!"

2. Q: How do we know that Adam was gay?
   A: Because he had Eve and an apple and he ate the apple.

3. The Bible professor dropped the stack of essays on the desk and looked into the sea of anxious faces.

   "Everyone passed," he said, "with the exception of O'Dolin."

   The young student looked up with genuine surprise. "Professor," he said, "I thought my paper on Jesus was revolutionary!"

   "That it was," the professor agreed, "though I hardly consider it 'proof' that Jesus was Jewish simply because he went into his father's business, lived at home until he was thirty, and had a mother who thought he was God. . . ."

4. Then, of course, there was the seminarian who

argued that Noah had the best hearing in the Bible. When asked to back up his claim, he pointed out that it was God Himself who insisted that Noah herd everything. . . .

5. "I have good news, and I have bad news," spake Moses as he returned from the peaks of Mt. Sinai. "The good news is that God has reduced the commandments to ten. The bad news is that adultery's still in."

BIGAMY   See also INFIDELITY, MARRIAGE

1. According to some who you talk to, bigamy and monogamy are the same thing: one wife too many.

2. What is singular about the bigamist, however, is that he keeps two himself. . . .

BIRTH CONTROL   See also PREGNANCY, SEX, and DOCTORS 10, SCHOOL 5

1. Q: What's the difference between a condom and a coffin?
A: Both contain stiffs, but the one in the condom is coming while the one in the coffin is going.

2. Q: Why is a pebble in a man's shoe the most effective means of birth control?

   A: Because it makes him limp.

3. Then there was the tea manufacturer who had a dozen kids because of his flow-through bags. . . .

4. Walking up to the druggist, slow-on-the-uptake Irving said, "I'm rather new at this. How much, my good man, for a box of condoms?"

   The pharmacist replied, "They're $4.95 plus $.37 for tax."

   "Ah," said Irving, "I always wondered how you keep them on."

5. Then there was the wily young man who convinced women to fight one bird with another: The best way to keep the stork at bay was with a swallow.

6. Newlywed Mrs. Hefner walked into the gynecologist's office, a long expression on her face.

   "What seems to be the problem?" Dr. Abramowicz enquired as he helped her onto the table.

   "Doctor, ever since you fit me with the diaphragm, I've been urinating purple."

   "Hmmmm . . . that *is* strange. What kind of jelly are you using?"

   "Grape," she responded.

7. Then there was the man who made a good living selling custom-made diaphragms at fifty dollars a crack.

BIRTHDAYS

See also DERELICTS 1

1. You know you've lived a good, long life when they put the cake ingredients in a pan, light the candles, and the cake cooks itself.

2. "Well, Billy," said the young boy's parents, "what would you like for your birthday?"

Thinking hard, he said, "I wanna watch." So on the night of his birthday, they let him.

3. "Perhaps," said the clerk to his customer, "your wife might like some cucumber soap for her birthday?"

"I don't think so," replied the husband. "She just rinses 'em off with water."

4. The man walked over to the perfume counter and told the clerk he'd like a bottle of Chanel No. 5 for his wife's birthday.

"A little surprise, eh?" smiled the clerk.

"You bet," answered the customer. "She's expecting a cruise."

5. Emma said proudly, "My great-grandfather

doesn't drink, smoke, eat red meat, philander with women, gamble, or even swear. And tomorrow he's going to celebrate his ninety-seventh birthday."

Jason looked at her and asked, "How?"

6. Upon receiving a comb made of solid gold for his birthday, the grateful Hans told his wife, "Thanks, I'll never part with it."

BISEXUALS

See also HOMOSEXUALS, TRANSVESTITES

1. Bisexual men are easy to please, since they like girls as well as the next guy. . . .

2. Of course, when most men learn that they're bisexual, it's usually quite a blow.

BLACKMAIL

1. "Hey, Mom," asked Ralph. "will you lend me five dollars?"

"Certainly not."

"If you do," he went on, "I'll tell you what dad said to the maid when you were at the beauty shop."

The woman's ears perked and, grabbing her pocketbook, she handed over the money. "Well? What did he say?"

"He said, 'Hey, Marion—make sure you do my socks tomorrow.'"

BLINDNESS   *See also* DEAFNESS and CLOTHING 2

1. Q: What's the nastiest gift that can be given a blind person?
   A: A paint-by-numbers set.

2. Q: What's the nastiest gift a blind person can give?
   A: The painting.

3. Then there were the fraternity jokers who played a trick on their blind brother by leaving the plunger in the toilet. . . .

4. Q: What's the theme song for two blind people playing tennis?
   A: "Endless Love."

5. Q: Why do blind people masturbate with one hand?
   A: So they can moan with the other.

6. Then there was the blind person whose favorite color was corduroy.

7. Q: What goes, "Click, click, click, click, did I get it? Click, click, click, click, did I get it?"
   A: A blind person playing with Rubik's Cube.

8. The blind man was out walking with his Seeing Eye dog when suddenly the animal paused and wet the blind man's leg. Bending down, the blind man stretched out his hand and patted the dog's head.

   Having watched what happened, a passerby said, "Say, why are you patting him? That dog just peed on your leg!"

   "I know," said the blind man, "but I gotta find his head before I can kick his ass."

9. Finally reaching his destination, the bookstore, the blind man picked up his Seeing Eye dog by the hind legs and swung it up and down.

   Stunned, the clerk came over and asked, "C-can I help you, sir?"

   "No," replied the blind man. "Just browsing."

10. The woman had just stepped into the bathtub when the doorbell rang.

   "Who is it?"

   "Blind man," come the response.

   Feeling charitable, the woman dashed from

the tub without bothering to put on any clothes, grabbed her purse, and opened the door.

The man's jaw dropped and he stammered, "Wh-where do you want me to put these blinds, lady?"

BOATS   *See also* SAILING

1. After much deliberation the boatbuilder decided to start making all his ships from kosher wood. It was the only way to make sure they wouldn't tip.

BOOKS   *See also* LIBRARIANS and BLINDNESS, 9
                                    MOTION PICTURES 3

1. Shrinkwrapped, the book *Twenty Ways to Mate: Translated from the French with Original Illustrations*, was selling like hotcakes. As he rang up yet another sale, one clerk shook his head and said to another, "You know, I've just never seen a chess book sell so well!"

See also BASEBALL, FOOTBALL, GOLF, HOCKEY, SOCCER, WRESTLING, and ADVERTISING 1

1. Telling his grandson about his days as a Golden Gloves contestant, Max said, "The bell rang, and we met in the center of the ring. First he threw a left cross, then came the right cross."

   Max hesitated and his grandson said, "Then what happened?"

   "Then," sighed Max, "came the Red Cross."

2. Max went on, "But by the third round I had my opponent worried."

   "Did you really?" his grandson pressed.

   "You bet. He thought he'd killed me."

3. Which wasn't quite as bad as the fighter who was deadly with a rabbit punch. Unfortunately, they made him fight people.

4. Wallace and Theodore were best of friends, and there was nothing they liked more than watching a good boxing match. Whether it was in person, on ESPN, or even over the radio, they enjoyed to the hilt the manly sport of pugilism.

"Wouldn't it be awful," Wallace said one day, "if when we die there's no boxing in Heaven?"

Theodore agreed that it would indeed be terrible, and the two men made a pact: Whoever died first would do his best to come back and tell the other whether there was boxing in the hereafter.

The very next day, as fate would have it, Theodore was hit by a car and died. That night the grieving Wallace was lying in his bed mourning when all of a sudden a familiar voice drifted from the ether.

"Wally . . . Wally, are you there?"

Wallace was suddenly alert. "Ted, is that you?"

"Yes, it's me. And I have good news and bad news."

"What's the good news?" Wallace asked urgently.

"There's boxing in Heaven," he said. "All the greats are here . . . Joe Louis, John L. Sullivan . . . and they're still fighting!"

"That's great! What's the bad news, then?"

"You and I both have ringside seats to Sunday's Marciano/Corbett fight."

1. Q: What is the motto of a gay scoutmaster?
   A: From every young scout a grown man will emerge.

2. Q: What's blue and comes in brownies?
   A: Cub Scouts.

BUILDERS   See also ROYALTY 7

1. Mr. Straub stood in the bedroom of the house he'd just built.

   "I don't care whether you believe me or not," Mrs. Feinstein said, "but each time a train enters the station, the bed shakes so bad I fall out."

   Checking his watch, Straub said, "There's a train due in just a minute. Do you mind if I see for myself?"

   Not objecting in the least, Mrs. Feinstein pointed out which side was hers, and Mr. Straub lay down. Moments later, Mr. Feinstein walked in.

   "Hey," he bellowed, "just what do you think you're doing?"

"Would you believe," said the builder, "waiting for a train?"

2. "Jesus," Mike said to Steven at the construction job, "you've been working hard today!"

Steven winked. "I'm just foolin' the boss. Been carrying the same load of bricks up and down the stairs all day!"

3. The two men drove up to the lumberyard, but only one of them got out. He was an apprentice builder and was making his first buy on his own.

He walked up to the clerk and announced, "I'd like some four-by-fours."

The clerk eyed the young man suspiciously. "You mean two-by-fours, don't you?"

The apprentice shook his head. "I'm sure my boss said four-by-fours."

"Is that him in the car?" the clerk said. "The apprentice nodded. "Do me a favor then and ask him exactly how long you want them."

Shrugging, the novice went over to the car. When he returned, he said to the clerk,, "We're building a house; we want them forever."

4. But the apprentice refused to be discouraged. Handed a set of plans, he went to the person's house and began work on the new chimney.

Two days later, the contractor came over to see how he was doing; much to his surprise, the brick structure towered nearly a quarter-mile over the house.

Stomping over to the apprentice, he demanded to know what he was doing.

"I was just following the plans," the youth said defensively.

"Schmuck!" the contractor cried, turning the plans over, "you were supposed to build a well!"

BUSINESS See also FINANCE, THE OFFICE, and DEATH 2, DRINKING 3, POSTAL WORKERS 4

1. "Power lunches are passé," said one business-person to another. "Today, the fashionable meal is the economy lunch."

"You mean brown-bagging it?" asked his companion.

"No, I mean beef broth for an appetizer and mince pie for dessert. It's called making both ends meat."

2. Then there was the CEO whose bonus was up to six big figures: the board of trustees.

3. The senior VP shuffled into his house and was greeted by his wife.

"Ralph," she said, startled, "what are you doing home so early?"

"The boss and I had a fight," he grumbled. "He wouldn't take back what he said."

Beaming with pride, the woman asked, "What did he say?"

The senior VP shrugged. "You're fired."

4. "How long have you been working here?" one employee said to another.

"Ever since the boss threatened to fire me."

5. "I'll have you know," said the snob to his date, "my father is a prominent man in this town. He's a Lion . . . a Moose . . . *and* an Elk."

"Wow!" said the young woman, "and what do you charge to see him?"

6. "Always remember," said the businessman to his son, "there are two things that will ensure your success in business."

"What are they?"

The businessman said in a stentorian voice, "Integrity and wisdom."

"Integrity?"

"That's right. No matter how it may be to your detriment, no matter what your colleagues or the board may say, *always* keep your word once you have given it."

"And wisdom?"

"Don't be a horse's ass and give it."

7. Then there was the floundering businesswoman

who turned to the Bible for solace. Her luck: She opened right to Chapter Eleven.

8. As a show of love, business partners Richard and Stanford agreed that whoever died first, the other would put five thousand dollars cash in his coffin. As it happened, when Stanford died Richard was so distraught that he made the check out for ten thousand dollars.

BUTCHERS   *See also* FOOD and INFLATION 3

1. "I'd like two pork chops," said the patron to her butcher, "and make them lean."
   "Yes ma'am," said the obliging butcher, standing them on end. "Which way?"

2. "Do you sell dog's meat?" asked the woman in the butcher shop.
   The butcher replied, "Sure . . . as long as the owners pay."

3. When he was in India, Mr. Wilson had tasted monkey brains. He found them so delectable that each and every day he stopped by the butcher shop to ask for them. And each day the butcher's reply was the same: "Sir, we just don't carry monkey brains!"
   Finally, after a week of this, the butcher be-

came exasperated beyond words. "Look," he said when Mr. Wilson came in for the eighth time, "if you took the *book* out of *bookworm*, what would you have?"

Mr. Wilson thought for a moment. "Worm," he replied.

"Right. And if you took the *type* out of *typewriter*, what would you have then?"

"Writer," Mr. Wilson answered.

"Exactly. So what would you have if you took the *frig* out of *monkey brains*?"

Mr. Wilson scratched his head. "Hey, wait a minute! There's no *frig* in *monkey brains*."

The butcher shot back, "That's exactly what I've been trying to tell you all week!"

CANNIBALS

See also NATIVES
and UNDERTAKERS 4

1. One cannibal said to the other, "You know, I really can't stand my wife."

"To hell with her, then," said the other. "Just eat the noodles."

2. One must acknowledge the missionary who gave the Mbutu cannibals their first taste of Christianity. . . .

3. Then there was the vengeful cannibal who ate someone that disagreed with him.

4. After being captured by cannibals, the hunter was stripped and lashed to a stake in the center of the village. Thereafter, every time the cannibals had a meal, they went to the hunter, poked him with a spear, and washed their food down with his blood.

Following several days of this, the hunter called over the chief of the tribe.

"Kill me," gasped the bound man, "eat me," he went on, "but for God's sake I've had it being stuck for the drinks."

5. The missionary arrived in the cannibal settlement on Monday, and by Tuesday afternoon he was history. Looking through his belongings, one of the natives found a magazine and without missing a beat began tearing out pictures of people and popping them in his mouth.

Seeing what he was doing, one of his friends asked, "So—how's the dehydrated stuff?"

6. Then there was the cannibal who went to a shrink because he was fed up with people.

7. That cannibal had a brother whose problem was physical rather than psychological: Every time he ate a missionary, he threw up. After several months of vomiting, he went to the local witch doctor, who diagnosed the case thusly: "It just goes to show that you can't keep a good man down."

8. The cannibal chief accepted an invitation to visit America, but after a few days of hamburgers and hot dogs he was desperate for a taste from home.

Having agreed to be interviewed by a newspaper, he asked the reporter, "What is your title at office?"

"Why, I'm travel editor," the journalist replied.

Licking his lips, the cannibal leader said, "How you like to be editor in chief?"

9. Then there was the young cannibal who went to school, ate his schoolmates, and passed the class.

10. Which was worse than the frugal cannibal who only ate at restaurants which advertised, "Children half-price."

CARD GAMES

See also GAMBLING

1. Concerned about all of her sisters who were tricked or cajoled into playing strip poker, the feminist clothes designer came up with stockings that could be taken off in a dozen pieces. She called it ante hose. . . .

2. Of course, strip poker is the only game in which

the more you lose, the more you have to show for it.

3. After his divorce Mr. Jones realized that poker isn't the only game that starts with holding hands and ends with a staggering financial loss.

4. Mr. Gregg had the boys over for poker but, as fate would have it, his wife had to work late that night, and he had to keep an eye on their eleven-year-old-son, Bruce.

Bruce was a curious lad, and all night long he did nothing but float around the table, reading each man's hand and muttering the contents to himself . . . loud enough for everyone to hear. Each time, Mr. Gregg would usher his son to another room, but despite frequent entreaties and even more frequent threats Bruce always returned to the den. Finally, one of the players got so fed up that he took Bruce by the elbow and led him away. When he returned, the game resumed; five minutes passed, then ten, then a half-hour, and not once did young Bruce show his face.

Amazed, Mr. Gregg asked, "Hell, Spike, what did you do—*kill* the kid?"

"Shit, no," he replied. "I taught him how to jerk off."

5. Warren came home after a late-night poker game and was greeted by his nagging, sourpussed wife.

"And just where have *you* been all night?"

"Playing cards," he said, "but that's not important. What matters is that I lost you to Roger Kaputnik."

"Lost me!!" she screamed. "How did you manage that?!"

"It was a heartbreaker," he admitted. "I had to fold with a royal flush."

6. Mr. Ecco was a narcissist's narcissist: His favorite game was strip solitaire.

CATS   *See also* ANIMALS, DOGS, PETS

1. Because he spent the nights howling as he made love to one svelte kitten or another, the aggressive tomcat Studd was a source of irritation to the neighborhood. Thus, Mr. Essoe reluctantly took the proud cat to be neutered.

A few days later, one of the neighbors happened to meet Mr. Essoe in the street. The men apologized for the inconvenience each had caused the other, after which the neighbor tried to lighten the conversation.

"Yeah," he said, "it's been a rough time, but I'll bet ole Studd's probably leading a more relaxed life now, just lyin' around and gettin' fat."

"Quite the contrary," Mr. Essoe replied with

a trace of pride. "He's still out each night, only now he goes as a consultant."

2. A technology buff, Mel spent hours poring over the ad in *Popular Engineering* for a ball-bearing mousetrap. He tried to figure out how it could possibly work, then finally gave up and sent for one. A week later, a tomcat arrived via parcel post.

3. Tired of having to stare at the luscious young kitten on the other side of the chain link fence, bold Tommy Tomcat decided to visit her one day. Settling back on his haunches, he gave a mighty leap and landed on the other side; impressed, the lovely cat sauntered over.

"That was quite a leap," she remarked. "Want to go somewhere and cuddle?"

" 'Fraid not," said Tommy, a pained expression on his face. "The fence was higher than I thought."

4. Then there was the gambling tomcat who put everything he had into the kitty.

5. "Julie!" screamed her mother, "why are you feeding birdseed to the cat?"

"I have to," Julie replied. "That's where my canary is."

6. Q: What's the difference between a phrase and a cat?

A: One has a pause at the end of its clause. . . .

7. Heloise stormed into the pet shop and confronted the owner. "I want to return this cat. You said it was good for mice, but all it does is lie there."

"So," the proprietor replied, "isn't that good for mice?"

8. Mr. Kelley walked anxiously to the door of the house and knocked. When a sweet old lady answered, he said nervously, "I'm sorry, madam, but I have some bad news. I'm afraid I've run over your cat. I . . . I'd like to replace it."

The old woman looked him up and down and said, "I'm game, but how are you at catching mice?"

CHARITY

1. Mr. Jacobson decided to take a week off from the pressures of the office and went skiing. Alas, no sooner did he reach the slopes than he heard an ominous rumbling; moments later a sheet of snow came crashing toward him. Fortunately, Mr. Jacobson was able to jump into a cave just before the avalanche hit. Just as fortunately, he had matches with him and was able to light a fire.

Hours later, when everyone but Mr. Jacobson had returned, a rescue team was sent to search for him. After several hours they saw smoke curling from the cave and went to investigate. Poking his head into the entrance, one of the rescuers yelled, "Mr. Jacobson, are you there? It's the Red Cross."

Bristling, the harried executive called back, "Get lost, dammit! I gave at the office!"

CHAUVINISM   See also FEMINISM
                                 and BABIES 1, POLICE 6

1. Q: What's a chauvinist's idea of a tragedy?
   A: A NOW bus going over a cliff—with four empty seats.

2. One chauvinist complained to the other, "Used to be that the first person a woman talked to about having a baby was her husband. Now it's her boss."

3. Then there was the chauvinist who actually *approved* of feminism. "Yeah," he told a friend, "women used to kiss me on the lips, but it's all over now."

4. "My wife is an idiot to want equal rights," said the henpecked chauvinist. "She'd be miserable with so few."

5. Then there was the chauvinist who was against capital punishment because he didn't think women would be hung like men.

6. Following a whirlwind romance and marriage, Beverly and Sid came back to reality . . . and a sobering reality it was for them.

   After making love one night, Sid threw Beverly his pants. "Here," he said, "try them on."

   The woman did so and, standing beside the bed, said, "They're much too big."

   "You got it," Sid replied. "I never want you to forget just who wears the pants in this house."

   Scowling, Beverly reached down, plucked her panties from the bed, and tossed them at her husband. "Try them on," she ordered.

   Studying the garment, Sid snickered, "Forget it! I'll never get into these!"

   Beverly headed for the bathroom. "Until your attitude changes," she said over her shoulder, "that's absolutely right."

CHESS   *See also* BOOKS 1

1. It was the middle of a championship game, and Kaspovsky was studying the board. All of a sudden his opponent, Nevsky, sneezed.

   "Bless you," said Kaspovsky.

   Nevsky looked up angrily. "Did you come here to play or to talk?"

2. Q: What's the difference between a chess player and a civil servant?
   A: A chess player moves every now and then.

3. Then there was the gay lad who gave up chess as soon as he discovered that now and then queens were sacrificed.

4. "Did you hear?" one Russian asked another. "Stakovsky died after losing the chess championship to an American."
   "Died!" he exclaimed. "When?"
   "Tomorrow."

CHRISTMAS

See DOGS, 6, MILLIONAIRES 4, POSTAL WORKERS 3

1. The clergy is concerned about the lack of religion in Christmas. According to an unofficial survey, the only time most people mention God is when they check the price tags.

2. Then there was the pundit who pointed out that the slogan he saw most frequently on Christmas was not "Peace on Earth" or "God Rest Ye Merry Gentlemen," but "Batteries Not Included."

3. Winking at a streetcorner Santa and asking him

for a luscious blonde, Mr. Roy was surprised when Mrs. Roy promised he was going to get it.

4. Not that Santa Clauses have it easy. The Santa Clause at Macy's has water on the knee . . . at least a dozen times a day.

5. The minister glared down at Mr. Foster and roared, "And are you, my son, a soldier in the army of the Lord?"

Surprised at being singled out, Mr. Foster replied anxiously, "Y-yes sir, I am."

"Then why," pressed the clergyman, "do we see you here *only* at Christmas."

Thinking quickly, Mr. Foster replied, "Would you believe, sir, I'm in the secret service?"

CIRCUMCISION *See also* RELIGION 2

1. Because he was a little careless when he circumcised the baby, Dr. Blum left the parents no choice but to skirt the issue. . . .

1. After years of being blasted into a net, the human cannonball went to the circus owner and told him he was going to retire.

    "But you can't!" shouted the cigar-chomping boss. "Where am I going to find a man of your caliber?"

2. As it turned out, the human cannonball who replaced him was hired and fired the same night.

3. Then there was the sad saga of the lady contortionist who was unable to have a satisfactory relationship because men were afraid she'd break it off. . . .

4. Q: What's the difference between circus midgets and a women's track team?

    A: One is a bunch of cunning runts. . . .

5. The circus had come to town, and as usual the circus people paraded through town upon their arrival. There were clowns handing out balloons and jugglers tossing everything from bowling pins to baseballs. And bringing up the rear were the elephants, three of them marching in a line,

each with its trunk wrapped around the tail of the pachyderm before it.

Sadly, as the elephants were crossing the train tracks, a freight train came through at excessive speed. The first two elephants managed to get across the track, but the third was struck head-on.

Several days later the freight company got a bill for three dead elephants. Phoning the circus owner, the insurance agent said, "What kind of scam is this? Only one of your elephants was killed."

"That's true," agreed the carny boss, "but you ripped the assholes from the other two."

6. Always on the lookout for a sideshow attraction, the circus magnate was delighted when an aide told him he had a special visitor: a woman with a talking sheep. He ordered that they be admitted at once.

The slender young woman walked into the trailer, tugging a frightened sheep on a leash.

The carny boss eyed it dubiously as he chomped down on a stubby cigar. "So, your lamb talks. What does it say?"

"It says its name, sir."

The circus owner asked to hear it and, after some coaxing, the sheep muttered a timid. "Baaa. . . ."

Grinding his cigar in an ashtray, the carny boss complained, "I thought you told me it could say its name!"

"Baaa did," the woman protested.

7. Holmes left his wife outside the trailer of the circus manager and, hitching up his confidence, carried the two small cages inside. He emerged less than a minute later, his face a map of despair.

"He turned us down," Holmes told his wife.

"I don't believe it. You showed him the act?" Holmes nodded.

"You had Morty the Mouse play "The Minute Waltz" on the piano and Carla the Canary sing "The Queen of the Night" aria from *The Magic Flute*?"

Holmes nodded again.

"Then why wouldn't he hire them?"

Holmes sighed. "I took them out of the cages, and he saw right away that Carla's a fake and Morty's a ventriloquist."

CITY LIFE

1. Unlike suburbanites, city-dwellers don't walk for their health: They run.

2. Then there's the city where crime has gotten so bad that citizens figure muggings into their budgets.

3. "It isn't that I don't like the city," explained the man as he went looking for a house in the suburbs. "I just wish they collected the garbage as often as they collect my taxes."

CLERGY　　　　　　　　*See also* THE BIBLE, HEAVEN,
　　　　　　　　　　　　　　RELIGION, and ANIMALS 11,
　　　　　　　　　　CANNIBALS 2, 5, CHRISTMAS 1, 5
　　　　　　　　　DEAFNESS 2, DOGS 8, HOMOSEXUALS 14,
　　　　　HYPNOTISM 1, LAWYERS 1, MASTURBATION 3, 4,
　　　　　　　　　　　　　　　POLITICS 4, SUICIDE 2

1. After his annual inspection of the local covent,
   the bishop approached the mother superior.
   　"It's my sad duty to inform you," he said
   glumly, "that during our tour we found a case of
   gonorrhea."
   　Her eyes wide, the mother superior exclaimed,
   "Praise the Lord! I was getting tired of Chianti!"

2. One hotel bellhop sighed to another, "I hate
   these rabbinical conventions! The rabbis bring a
   ten-dollar bill and the Ten Commandments—and
   they don't break either of them."

3. Q: What does the pope have in common with a
   Christmas tree?
   　A: Both have balls just for decoration.

4. The priest and the rabbi were sharing a hotel
   room at a convention of clergy members. As
   they climbed into their beds, the rabbi said

wistfully, "Tell me, Father, have you ever eaten pussy?"

Shocked, the priest snapped, "Certainly not! Why, that would be like you eating ham!"

The rabbi lay back and smiled. "Maybe, but I'll tell you this: There's no comparison."

5. Q: Why doesn't the pope like to take a shower?
A: He hates looking down on the unemployed.

6. The young girl said to the rather hip priest, "Father, is it a sin to have sex before receiving Communion?"

He replied, "Only if you block the aisle."

7. The clergyman said to the Sunday school class, "And do you know, my children, where bad little boys and girls go?"

"Yes, sir," piped up one young lad, "behind the old mill by the river."

8. Then there was the parishioner who lost faith when his priest announced that the end was near . . . just before asking the congregation to commit to a two-year building pledge.

9. Oskar was dying of a rare form of flu, and as he lay on his deathbed he asked his wife to fetch a priest.

"A priest?" she said from the safety of the

next room. "Oskar, we've been Orthodox Jews all our lives."

"I know," he countered, "but you want I should make our rabbi sick?"

10. Then there was the congregation that was asked for money so often they insisted their pastor refer to them not as the flock but as the fleeced.

11. One of the members, Mr. Tweed, went so far as to try and find out if there really was a God. At church one Sunday he dropped a bill in the collection plate: The bill was for his son's college tuition.

12. Then there was the saint who taught her dog to heal. . . .

13. Q: What did the priest do when Jesus Christ came strolling toward him?
A: Tried to look busy.

14. The white missionary had done a great deal to bring religion to the black natives, especially in the area of premarital sex. Now none of the village girls was sleeping with any village boys unless they were married.

One day, however, a young wife gave birth to a white baby, and, furious, the chief of the village came to see the missionary.

"Father Holland," he said, "you have taught

us about the holiness of husband and wife love, yet today M'Bwee gave birth to a white child. Since you are the only white man in our village, the people are angry. They say *you* must be the father!"

Smiling benignly, Father Holland placed his arm around the chief's shoulder.

"Chief N'Gala," said the priest, "the baby is not mine, it's an albino." He pointed to a meadow where there was one black sheep and a dozen white. "It's like that black sheep out there—a fluke of nature, something that just happens now and then."

Shifting nervously from foot to foot, the chief said, "Say no more, Father Holland. I won't tell them about M'Bwee if you won't tell them about sheep."

15. Young Father O'Reilly, newly ordained, was to hear his first confessions. Anxious to get his ministry off on the right foot, he asked the experienced Father McMartin to sit in and critique his handling of the assignment.

At the end of the day the two clergymen sat in the rectory and reviewed O'Reilly's performance.

"Not bad," McMartin said, with a catch in his voice. Weighing his words with care, he went on, "But there *is* one thing. In the future, I think you should make an effort to say 'I understand' instead of 'Oh, wow!'"

16. The young woman came to see her priest about a problem she'd had and, looking at the stunning lass as she entered his study, the clergyman was filled with overwhelming lust. As she sat down, he was barely able to speak.

"What seems to be the problem?" he managed, sliding his chair next to hers.

"Father," she said quietly, "something happened when I went out on a date last night. He w-was very handsome, and . . . and. . . ."

The girl's voice drifted off, and, seeing an opening, the priest said, "Let me see if I can help you. Did he do this?" he asked, slipping his arm around her.

She nodded.

"And this?" he asked, kissing her passionately.

She nodded again.

Undressing her, he asked, "And this?"

Once again she nodded.

Taking off his clothes, the priest began to make love to her. "And . . . did he do *this*?" he asked, panting.

The young woman nodded.

Finishing with the woman, the priest sat back. "He did all of that?" he asked.

"That," she confided, "and more."

"More?" the priest exclaimed. "How could he have done more?"

"He gave me the clap," she replied.

17. Before they could be ordained, the three young

men had to undergo an ordeal which would test the chastity of their thoughts. Ordered by a priest to strip, the trio had rubber bands fastened to their private parts and were ushered into a bedroom where a beautiful girl lay naked on the bed.

After a few moments a loud *"boing"* was clearly heard, and the first seminarian was told to go to the showers to cool his ardor. A moment later a second *"boing"* rang out, and the owner of that rigid member was also sent to the showers. Minutes passed, and when nothing happened to the third aspiring clergyman, he was congratulated by the priest.

"Well done, my son," he enthused. "Now go and join the others in the shower."

"Boing!"

18. Pope John Paul II granted one of his rare interviews, and the journalist began by asking the pontiff if he had any pet peeves.

"Only two," he said candidly. "Firstly, I dislike Polish jokes because they portray Poles as ignorant oafs; and secondly, I can no longer abide M & M's."

The reporter looked up from her notebook. "I understand the Polish jokes, Your Holiness, but . . . why do you hate M & M's?"

The pope replied, "Because I don't like having to peel off the shells to get to the chocolate."

19. Then there was the pastor who rehearsed his sermons over and over before delivering them. He was, in short, a man who practiced what he preached.

CLOTHING *See also* TAILORS and BALLERINAS 1, CARD GAMES 1, 2, DREAMS 3, SALESPEOPLE 3

1. Sitting at the bar and admiring the young girl tucked into her skin-tight jeans, the single gentleman asked, "You've got to tell me, miss, how anyone gets into those pants."

"Well," she smiled, "he starts by buying me a drink."

2. When Mr. Jameson died, he left behind a very unhappy haberdasher who had made the eccentric millionaire a plaid three-piece suit.

"I'll tell you what," the haberdasher told his assistant Ernie, "if you can sell this suit, I'll let you keep half the money."

Taking the garment home with him, he remembered blind old Herbie who lived in his building and convinced him to buy the suit.

The next morning Ernie came to work all bruised and cut up.

"Dear God!" cried the haberdasher, "what happened to you?"

"Well," Ernie replied, "I sold the suit to a blind neighbor . . . and man, was his Seeing Eye dog pissed!"

3. Watching her mother as she tried on her new fur coat, young Becky said unhappily, "Mom, do you realize some poor dumb beast suffered so you could have that?"

The woman shot her an angry look. "Becky, how dare you talk about your father like that!"

4. As the bus pulled up, Angie realized she was going to have a difficult time getting on. Her dress was too tight for her to step up, her hands were full of packages, and the line of people behind her did not seem to be in a charitable mood.

She realized that the best thing to do was to try to loosen her dress so, with great effort, she stretched her hand behind her and pulled the zipper down halfway. When that didn't seem to help, she pulled it down the rest of the way.

Just then the bus pulled up and, still unable to ascend, she was both shocked and offended when a man standing behind her picked her up and put her on the bus.

Turning, she growled, "What right did you have to touch me?"

The man climbed on and said, "Well, after you pulled my fly down I kind of figured we were good friends."

5. Then .there was the furrier who, for a very special client, crossed a mink with a gorilla to produce a unique garment. The fur was spectacular, but, alas, the sleeves were too long.

6. Dating the first southern girl he'd ever known, the Yankee was surprised when she greeted him at the door in the lowest-cut gown he'd ever seen.

"Th-that's a lovely dress," he stuttered, his eyes on her ample bosom.

"Sho' nough," she replied.

To which he answered, "I'll say!"

7. "And if I didn't wear a halter top and tight jeans," asked the girl, "would you still find me appealing?"

"Let's find out," the man replied gamely.

8. As they were walking down the street, the young woman said to her lover, "Why won't you buy me a fur coat? I'm so cold."

Her boyfriend sniffed, "If you knew the answer, why'd you bother asking?"

9. As they were undressing in the locker room prior to a vigorous hour of racquetball, Ken was surprised to see Vinnie slip off a pair of women's panties.

"Say, old shoe," he said, "I hope you don't

think I'm being too personal, but—when did you start wearing ladies' underwear?"

Vinnie replied, "Ever since my wife found them in my glove compartment."

10. The rather liberal young lady came home from the store and showed her husband the new dress she'd bought, which was made of plastic and totally transparent.

"But honey," the young man gasped, "people will see right through it!"

"No they won't, dummy," she replied. "I'll be inside of it."

11. Then there was the teenage girl who glibly referred to her maternity dress as a slip cover.

COLLEGE   *See also* SCHOOL and ANATOMY 1, ANTIQUES 2, BASEBALL 3, THE BIBLE 3, BLINDNESS 3, CLERGY 11, FEMINISM 3, FOOTBALL 6, LAWYERS 7, HOMOSEXUALS 7, PARTIES 2, SEX 20

1. Then there was the student who got good grades because she had a faculty for lovemaking.

2. There was the coed who decided to write a thesis about sex in the faculty and found herself working under several great minds.

3. "As you can see, class," said the medical school professor pointing to the X-ray, "this patient limps because his left fibia and tibula are both radically arched. Johnson—what would you do in a case like this?"

"Well, ma'am," said the student, "I suppose I'd limp, too."

4. Then there was the college that had the reputation of being a fountain of knowledge where everyone went to drink.

5. Listening to the commencement address by the new dean, Professor Papp turned to a woman sitting beside him.

"Can you believe that the trustees named someone so ugly to be our new dean?"

Stiffening, the woman said, "I beg your pardon, but do you know who I am?"

Turning to study her, the professor replied, "Can't say I do."

"I'll have you know that I am that ugly man's wife!"

Drawing himself erect, the professor shot back, "And do you know who *I* am?"

"I haven't had the pleasure," she said icily.

"Good," he replied, "then my job's still safe."

6. After years of controversy the university football coach finally had to agree that the school was placing too much emphasis on sports and

too little on education: Though every player on the team had a letter, only three of them knew which one it was.

7. Then there was the coed who got an A when her history teacher found that she was terrible on names but great on dates.

8. "Today," said the professor, "I will be lecturing about the liver and spleen."

Up in the gallery, one med student leaned toward the other, "Damn, if there's one thing I can't stand it's an organ recital."

9. The aspiring psychiatrists were attending their first class on emotional extremes.

"Just to establish some parameters," said the professor, "Mr. Nichols: What is the opposite of joy?"

"Sadness," said the student.

"And the opposite of depression, Ms. Biggs?"

"Elation."

"How about the opposite of woe, Mr. Wilson?"

"I believe that's giddyap," the student replied.

COMPUTERS   *See also* ACCOUNTANTS 4,
SALES PEOPLE 5

1. "This little computer," said the sales clerk, "will do half your job for you."

Studying the machine the senior VP decided, "Fine, I'll take two."

CONSTIPATION

1. Aged Dora Nathanson went to her doctor to see what could be done about her constipation.

"It's terrible," she said, "I haven't moved my bowels in a week."

"I see. Have you done anything about it?"

"Naturally," she replied, "I sit in the bathroom for a half-hour in the morning and again at night."

"No," the doctor said, "I mean do you take anything?"

"Naturally," she answered, "I take a book."

COOKING

See also FOOD

1. The foul smell of burning milk drew Herb into the kitchen, where his wife was standing over a steaming pot.

   "I've made clam chowder," Evie said.

   Herb sighed with relief. "Thank God. I thought *we* would have to eat it."

COWBOYS

1. More than anything, dull Dennis wanted to be a cowpoke. Taking pity on him, a rancher decided to hire the lad and give him a chance.

   "This," he said, showing Dennis a rope, "is a lariat. We use it to catch cows."

   "I see," said Dennis, trying to seem knowledgeable as he examined the riata. "And what do you use for bait?"

CRIME

See also JUDGES, JURIES, MURDER,
POLICE, PRISON,
and ACCOUNTANTS 1, 2, CITY LIFE 1, 2,
HOMOSEXUALS 4, SMALL TOWNS 2

1. The well-dressed businessman was walking down a dark street in New York's garment district when he was accosted by a mugger. Ordered to hand over all his money, the businessman did so, placing one hundred dollars in the mugger's open hand.

   When he'd surrendered all his money, the businessman casually retrieved two dollars and slipped them back into his money clip.

   The crook with disbelief, "What the hell are you doing?"

   The businessman replied, "I always take a two percent discount for cash transactions."

2. The judge glowered at the haggard robber and said, "Then you *admit* breaking into the same dress shop on four successive nights?"

   "Yes, your honor."

   "And why was that?"

   "Because my wife wanted a dress."

   The judge consulted his records. "But it says here you broke in four nights in a row!"

"Yes, sir. She made me exchange it three times."

3. Then there was the moron who went to the post office to mail a letter and ended up in jail. He saw a poster saying, "Man Wanted for Post Office Robbery" and took the job.

4. After hearing several thuds on the roof, Mr. Thomas looked out the window and saw the neighbor's son Jed with a rock in his hand. The youth was obviously trying to hit the big bay windows, and in a rage Mr. Thomas ran outside. He grabbed the boy just as he was about to let loose another projectile.

"So!" Mr. Thomas screamed, "I'll teach you to throw rocks at my windows!"

"Would you really?" the boy declared. "I keep missing."

5. The suspicious-looking man drove up to the border, where he was greeted by a sentry. When the guard looked in the trunk, he was surprised to find six sacks bulging at the seams.

"What's in here?" he asked.

"Dirt," the driver replied.

"Take them out," the guard instructed, "I want to check them."

Obliging, the man removed the bags, and, sure enough, each one of them contained nothing but dirt. Reluctantly, the guard let him go.

A week later the man came back, and, once again, the sentry looked in the trunk.

"What's in the bags this time?" he asked.

"More dirt," said the man.

Not believing him, the guard checked the sacks and, once again, he found nothing but soil.

The same thing happened every day for six months, and it finally became so frustrating to the guard that he quit and became a bartender. Then, one night, the suspicious-looking fellow happened to stop by for a drink. Hurrying over to him, the former guard said, "Listen, pal, drinks are on the house tonight if you'll do me a favor: Just tell me what the hell you were smuggling all that time."

Grinning broadly, the man leaned close to the bartender's ear and whispered, "Cars."

6. Then there was the town with a crime rate so high they didn't have an electric chair; they had an electric couch.

7. The Democratic party bigwig left his New York office to spy on the big Republican rally being held in Times Square. While he was there, a mugger put a gun to his head, forced him into an alley, and proceeded to rough him up while robbing him of everything he owned.

His clothes rumpled and brow covered with

sweat, he stumbled into Democratic headquarters, where his aides stared at him with shock.

"What happened?" asked his secretary as she handed him a glass of water. After he told them his frightening tale, the secretary asked, "Weren't there cops around?"

"Of course there were," he replied.

"Then why didn't you scream?"

"What?" he shot back. "And have the Republicans think I was cheering for them?"

8. Q: What's the difference between a pickpocket and a Peeping Tom?
   A: One snatches watches. . . .

9. Standing in line at the post office, the moron happened to notice wanted posters for two black men. Under the photos of both, it said "Wanted for Rape."

   "I know they're always complaining about discrimination," said the moron to his companion, "but I'll tell you—they manage to get the best jobs!"

10. Then there was Quincy, who got the chair. Every year his family lays a wreath on the fuse box.

11. The desperate mugger approached a bag lady and told her to hand over all her money. When she insisted she hadn't any, he thrust his hand

between her ample bosom and began feeling around.

"I said I didn't have any money," she repeated, "but if you keep that up, I'll be glad to write you a check."

12. The detective was interviewing the man whose clothing shop had just been burglarized.

"It's bad," said the proprietor, "but it's not as bad as it could have been if he'd robbed me yesterday."

"Why is that?" the detective asked.

"Because today everything was on sale."

13. Feeling nostalgic, the seventy-five-year-old Mr. Thomas drove with his wife to the nursery school where they'd first met. Outside, they stood before the old oak tree where he'd carved "JT loves ML" inside a heart; they peered into the windows at the corner where he'd stolen his first playful kiss from his future bride.

As they drove home, the Thomases found themselves behind an armored car; when the Brinks truck hit a pothole, a fat canvas bag dropped out, and the couple stopped to retrieve it.

"My God," said Mrs. Thomas, looking inside, "there must be half a million dollars in there."

Scrupulously honest, Mr. Thomas said, "Maisie . . . we must give it back."

"Like hell we will," she snapped, and they drove home.

The next day two insurance agents came to their door. "We're talking to all the people in the neighborhood," said one, "to see if they found a bag with money in it."

"No," said Maisie.

"Yes," replied her guilt-stricken husband.

Maisie fired him a withering glance, then said to the agents, "You'll have to excuse my husband . . . he's senile."

"No, I'm not," he insisted, holding the agents with a steady gaze. "Maisie and I were driving home from nursery school and— "

"Come on," said the agent to his associate, "let's go to the next house."

14. Then, of course, there was the town where criminals were *so* tough they attacked people with chewed-off shotguns. . . .

15. Then there was the Peeping Tom who was arrested, convicted, and given a bon voyeur party by his friends. . . .

CROSSWORD PUZZLES

1. Jim was doing the crossword puzzle on the train to work. As it happened, so was the commuter beside him as well as two nuns sitting behind them. After a while the man leaned over to Jim.

   "I see you're doing the puzzle. Did you happen to get thirty-two across?"

   "You mean the four-letter word meaning 'intercourse' and ending in a *k*?"

   "Yeah, that's the one."

   "Sure," said Jim. "The answer is *talk*."

   Behind him, one of the nuns said, "Excuse me, Sister Mary, but would you pass the eraser?"

2. Later in the ride, the man asked his wiser neighbor, "What's forty-two down, the four-letter word ending in *u-n-t* that means 'woman'?"

   Jim replied, "*Aunt*."

   Once again, the nun asked for an eraser.

1. Arriving at Lover's Lane, Charlie swung the car into the first spot he saw.

   Stunned, Anne said, "Charles, darling, why did you stop here? There are so many more scenic spots up the road."

   Sliding closer to his date, Charlie replied, "Because, Anne, I'm a firm believer in love at first site."

2. The young man was delighted when his date said she had a terrific night planned and that it would be on her. Then she paid for dinner, and his spirits plunged.

3. Q: Why should young people be careful when parking?
   A: Because accidents cause people.

4. It was only their first date, but the young lady was so delectable that her companion couldn't help but pinch her. When she looked at him and yelled, "Gross!" he grinned and did it 143 times more.

5. "We're going to have a terrific time tonight,"

said the young man when he arrived at his date's house. "I have three tickets to the concert."

"Three?" she replied. "Why do we need three?"

Winking slyly, the youth said, "They're for your parents and sister."

6. After hailing a cab, young Ryan boasted to the hack, "Yessir, it's going to be a great night. I met Jacqueline at the health club, and she invited me up to her apartment. She lives with her folks, but she said they'll be going to the ballet as soon as her dad gets home from work; after that, we'll have the apartment all to ourselves, and I intend to *party!*"

Arriving at the building and hurrying upstairs, the young man sat chatting with his date in the den while they waited for her father to arrive and her parents to leave.

Not long thereafter, the girl's parents entered the room. "Well," said Jacqueline's mother, "we'll be leaving now."

"Say," said Ryan. "I have a good idea. Why don't we go with you to the ballet?"

"Why how nice!" said Jacqueline's mother. "I'm sure we can buy two extra tickets."

As Ryan helped the disappointed Jacqueline on with her coat, she asked, "Why didn't you tell me you liked ballet?"

"Never mind that," Ryan replied. "Why didn't you tell *me* your old man drives a cab?"

7. Then there was the young man who was badly mauled fighting for his date's honor. She was trying to keep it.

8. The inexperienced young man was smitten with the girl who was sitting beside him in his parked car. Looking at her in the light of the full moon, he gently placed his hand on her knee and said, "Angie . . . I think I love you."

   With a knowing smile, she put her hand on his and said, "Higher, Ralph."

   Clearing his throat, he said, "Angie . . . I think I love you!" in a cracked falsetto.

9. Even less worldly was Warner. Not only was this his first date, but he was especially nervous because he knew that Sally had been around. Pretending to be gracious when in fact he had absolutely no idea what to do, Warner let her call the shots. At her suggestion they went to a hamburger place to eat, stopped at a disco to dance, and then went to an insolated beach that Sally had suggested.

   Feeling more confident as the night progressed, Warner was surprised when Sally said, "Hey . . . wanna go out on the beach and get naked?"

   Looking her straight in the eye, Warner said, "Hell, no, I want to stay here with you!"

10. Cuddling in the front seat of the car, Ernest

asked his date, "You don't shrink from kissing, do you?"

Jill replied, "If I did, I'd be awfully small by now."

11. Walking her to the door, Keith said to his date, "Will I see you pretty soon?"

"What's the matter," she asked, hurt. "Don't you think I'm pretty now?"

12. Then there was the young lady who insisted she hated staying out late, but her dates made her.

13. He was a determined young Frenchman: He kept after the girl until the *oui* hours of the morning. . . .

DEAFNESS   *See* BLINDNESS and FLATULENCE 4

1. Three nearly deaf friends met on a streetcorner.

"Isn't it windy?" the first asked the second.

"No," replied the second, "Thursday."

"Me, too," said the third with gusto. "Let's go get a beer."

2. Then there was the deaf seminary student who thought Moses had a wig because the Bible said he was sometimes seen with Aaron.

3. "I just purchased the most expensive hearing aid ever made," Stanely told his pal Joseph. "Imported from Sweden and guaranteed for life."

"How much did it cost?"

Stanley replied, "Five past two."

DEATH *See* GHOSTS, MURDER, SUICIDE, UNDERTAKERS, and BEER 3, BUSINESS 8, CLERGY 9, FIREFIGHTERS 2, FOOD 8, GOLF 3, 8, MOTHERS-IN-LAW 6, MOTION PICTURES 3, NEWSPAPERS 1

1. Burt and Ernie were best of friends, and, as they were both in their eighties, they made a bargain: Whoever died first would try hard to come back and tell the other what the afterlife was like.

Shortly after striking the deal, Ernie passed away. A few nights later Burt was lying in his bed when a voice wafted in through the open window.

"Burt . . . Burt. . . ."

The old man sat up. "My God! Ernie, is that you?"

"Yes . . . and I tell you, it's marvelous . . . simply marvelous."

"Tell me about it," Ernie urged, growing excited.

"Well . . . in the morning we eat breakfast

and then spend hours making love. Then we eat lunch and spend more hours making love. Finally, we eat dinner and make love again."

"Holy cow!" gushed Burt. "I can't *wait* to die and go to heaven!"

"Heaven?" retorted Ernie. "Hell, I'm outside. I came back as a rabbit."

2. "Jeremy," said the bedridden young man, "I—I can't die without telling you what a rotten partner I've been to you. I embezzled over a million dollars from the company, made a million more by selling secrets to our competition, and just to be spiteful I fired the receptionist because I knew she was in love with you."

"That's all right," said Jeremy softly. "I'm the one who poisoned you."

3. "David," said the glum-faced young man, "I'm so sorry! I just heard your Uncle Oscar fell from a cliff. Were you very close to him?"

"Just close enough to give him a push," answered David.

4. The police officer didn't know quite how to break the awful news to the woman. When she answered the doorbell, he said, "Mrs. Daniels, I'm Officer Smythe, and . . . you know that new fedora you bought your husband?"

"Yes . . . ?" she said.

"Well, it's been ruined."

"Ruined! How?"

The officer replied, "A safe fell on it."

5. The nurse burst into the doctor's office. "Dr. Hausen!" she yelled, "you just gave a clean bill of health to Mr. Schneer and . . . and he dropped dead right outside the door!"

The doctor leaped into action. "Quick," he said, "we've got to turn him around so it looks like he was just coming in!"

6. Mr. Belnick died on the golf course, and no one wanted to tell his wife. Finally Mr. Strassen agreed to make the call.

"Blanche," he said, "your husband lost five thousand dollars playing poker."

"What!" she screamed. "He should drop dead."

Mr. Strassen said, "Funny you should mention that. . . ."

DERELICTS

See POVERTY and CRIME 11

1. The bum approached the well-dressed man.

"Say, pal, couldja spare ten bucks for coffee?"

"Ten dollars!" the man exclaimed. "My dear fellow, not even in *this* city will you find an establishment that charges so much for coffee."

"I know," said the panhandler, "but it's my wife's birthday and I wanted t'knock off early."

2. Having collecting $1.30 from a day of panhandling, the bag lady went to the market and bought a peach. Still hungry, she bought another. Then a third. Her stomach continued to growl, and so, with the last of her day's take, she bought an apple. That finally hit the spot, and as she made her bed on a park bench she grumbled, "Damn. If I'd bought the apple first, I'd've had enough money left for a drink."

DIETS   See FAT

1. Mr. Noonan had a terrific idea for a weight-loss program, and he took out a newspaper ad announcing the first meeting. The ad had a photo of a delicious roast, enticing mounds of mashed potatoes smothered in butter, hot steaming buns, a bottle of wine, and a generous dishful of mousse. Beneath it was the line, "Come to our meeting, eat all you want, and lose weight."

Sure enough, hundreds of people showed up, paying fifty dollars each at the door. They stood around chatting, expressing amazement that they'd be able to eat all they wanted, and looked with keen anticipation at the food spread out on a table, everything from entrées to desserts.

Finally Mr. Noonan appeared. "Are you ready to begin?" he asked the slavering multitude.

"Yes!" came the unanimous reply.

"Terrific!" he shouted back, then said, "Ready
. . . set . . . eat your heart out!"

2. Mr. Schneider was terribly overweight, so his
doctor put him on a diet.

"I want you to eat regularly for two days, then
skip a day, and repeat this procedure for two
weeks. The next time I see you you should have
lost at least five pounds."

When Mr. Schneider returned, he shocked
the doctor by having dropped nearly twenty
pounds.

"Why, that's amazing!" the doctor said. "You
did this just by following my instructions?"

The slimmed-down Mr. Schneider nodded.
"I'll tell you, though, I thought I was going to
drop dead that third day."

"From hunger, you mean."

"No," replied Mr. Schneider, "from skipping."

DISEASES   *See* DOCTORS, EPILEPTICS,
                 HOSPITALS, LEPERS, and COLLEGE 3,
                      FARMERS 5, SEX 14, TRAVEL 2

1. Then there was the girl who caught syphilis in
a public lavatory; it was the most uncomfortable
fifteen minutes of her life.

2. The doctor told the none-too-swift Mr. Flynn,

"The only remedy certain to kill this kind of virus is plenty of orange juice."

"I see," Mr. Flynn said thoughtfully. "And how do I get them to drink it?"

3. "Your cough seems to be much better this morning," Dr. Gaines said to his patient.

"I should hope so," the patient replied, "I've been practicing all night."

4. Learning that he had a rare disease for which the only cure was a mother's milk, Mr. Shipman took out a personal ad to find a nursing mother. Much to his delight, a woman responded almost immediately, and, after agreeing on a price, he went to her apartment.

As it happened, Mr. Shipman had especially soft lips and an active tongue, and after five minutes of nursing the woman was beside herself with passion.

"Is there anything *else* I can offer you?" she panted.

Smiling impishly, Mr. Shipman replied, "If it's not too much trouble, do you happen to have any Oreos?"

5. Then there was the man whose vertigo was so severe that when he sneezed, people simply said, "*Gesund*."

6. Then there was the sex maniac who had asthma. He could only catch his breath in snatches.

7. The young man wrote in his diary, "March 12. My first day in Alaska has been terrific! I shot a polar bear and made love to an Eskimo girl." Alas, the entry for March 27 wasn't quite so sunny. "Bad news. The doctor said I'd be better off if I'd done March 12 the other way around."

8. "Tell me," said the intern to his patient, "do you suffer from hemorrhoids?"

The crusty patient barked, "Some doctor you're going to make! What *else* can you do with them?"

9. After Roger and his fiancée had taken their premarital examinations, the doctor called him into his office.

"I have good news, and I have bad news," he told the young man. "The good news is that your fiancée has syphilis."

"Man, if that's the good news, what could the bad news possibly be?"

The doctor replied, "She didn't get it from you."

10. Q: What do a stomach ache and medical insurance have in common?
A: They both make you feel ill at ease.

DIVORCE *See* INFIDELITY, MARRIAGE, and CARD GAMES 3, TWINS 1

1. It wasn't long after he made a five-footer during a match that the golfer's wife sued for divorce.

2. "Young woman," said the judge, "this court is going to see to it that you receive one thousand dollars a month in alimony."

   "Thanks," the husband spoke up, "and I'll try to give her a few bucks myself."

3. Then there were the guests at the wedding of the oft-married Mr. Tracy. Though they wished the bride and groom well, they took the precaution of postdating the checks.

4. Then there was the moron who learned that incest was when you slept with your relatives. So he divorced his wife before making love with her.

5. "Why the big smile?" Henderson asked Churchill when he arrived at the office.

   "Last night my wife ran off with my best friend."

   "Really? Do I know the guy?"

   "No," Churchill replied, "and neither do I."

DOCTORS

See DISEASES, GYNECOLOGISTS, HOSPITALS, OPTOMETRISTS, PROCTOLOGISTS, PSYCHIATRISTS and ANATOMY 2, CIRCUMCISION 1, COLLEGE 3, 8, CONSTIPATION 1, DEATH 5, DIETS 2, DISEASE 2, 3, DRINKING 8, FLATULENCE 1, FOOD 4, HOMOSEXUALS 5, IMMIGRANTS 1, 3, JOGGING 1, MARRIAGE 19, POLITICS 3, SENIOR CITIZENS 6, TAXES 3

1. Mr. Blyth was shaving one morning when the can of shaving cream slipped from his hand and struck the toilet seat, scraping it. Knowing how particular his wife was about the bathroom, Mr. Blyth quietly slipped downstairs, found some paint that was just the right color, and quickly repainted the seat.

   Late for work, he then hurried out, forgetting to leave a note about the seat. Thus, when his wife awoke and went to the bathroom, she found herself stuck to the seat.

   Unable to move, she sat there crying until her husband came home for lunch. Apologizing profusely, Mr. Blyth unscrewed the seat and helped his wife into bed, lying her face-down.

"What are we going to do?" she wailed, "I can't spend the rest of my life wearing a toilet seat!"

"Don't worry," answered her husband, "I'll call the doctor and see if he can help."

Putting in a call to the family physician, Mr. Blyth didn't tell him what had happened but explained that there was no way his wife could go to his office. Reluctantly, the doctor agreed to stop by on his way home.

When the physician arrived, Mr. Blyth ushered him into the bedroom, where his wife got on her hands and knees and displayed her entrapped buttocks.

Mr. Blyth asked, "Well, doctor, you see why I called. What do you think?"

Stroking his chin, the doctor said, "I think it's lovely, but why such a cheap frame?"

2. "Johnny, where have you been?" Dr. Bova screamed when the young man finally answered his phone. "I have bad news and then I have *terrible* news!"

Johnny moaned, "Bad news *and* terrible news? Good Lord, give me the bad news first."

"Well," said the physician, "the bad news is that you've only got twenty-four hours to live!"

"Ohmigod! Then what could the *terrible* news possibly be?"

The doctor answered quickly, "I've been trying to call you since yesterday!"

3. A doctor was walking down the hospital corridor when he was stopped by Nurse Smith.

"Excuse me," she said, "but why do you have a thermometer behind your ear?"

Grabbing the instrument, the doctor swore. "Damn, some asshole has my pen!"

4. "It's incredible," the young man told his physician, "but every time I sneeze I have an orgasm. What do you recommend?"

The doctor replied, "Black pepper."

5. "Doctor!" the frantic mother screamed into the telephone late one night, "my baby just ate an entire tube of K-Y Jelly! What should we do?"

After a moment's reflection the physician said, "If you really can't wait, call one of the all-night drugstores."

6. "Jim, you'd better brace yourself," said the doctor to his patient, "I've got bad news."

"What is it?" asked the slightly panicked young man.

The doctor said, "Jim, I hate to say it, but you've only got six months to live."

"Six months!" screamed the patient. "My God, what am I going to do?"

The doctor shrugged. "If I were you, I'd get married and move to Kansas. It'll be the longest six months of your life."

7. The young man went to the doctor, complaining of an awful lisp. Giving him a thorough examination, the doctor determined that his problem was the size of his member: It was so large that it was actually pulling his tongue off center. Performing an emergency operation, the physician shortened the organ and sent the man on his way.

Several weeks later, the patient returned, complaining that while his lisp was gone, his sex life had also gone down the tubes.

"I'd like my penis back," he said mournfully.

At this, the doctor looked him straight in the eye and said, "Thcrew you."

8. Then there was the old man who wanted to wake up each day with a song in his heart, so his cardiologist fitted him with an AM-FM pacemaker.

9. "Nurse," said the doctor, "would you please take Mr. Oliver's pulse?"

"Why?" demanded the patient, "doesn't she have one of her own?"

10. Visiting her family doctor, Mrs. Lord enquired, "Is it true that certain kinds of vegetables will stop a child from growing?"

"That depends," replied the physician, "on where you put the vegetables."

11. Then there was the doctor's wife who bought a bushel of apples so she'd have time to dally with her lover.

12. And let's not forget the patient who was so thickheaded that when told to strip to the waist, he took off his pants.

13. Not that doctors are especially bright or efficient. One had a patient who had to wait a month for the results of a test that said he had only a week to live.

14. Waking up in the middle of the night with terrible pains in his chest, Mr. Stock put in an emergency call to his doctor.
   "Doctor Gish," he gasped, "I—I need you to make a house call. Hurry, I'll tell you where to go."
   Unfortunately the annoyed Dr. Gish beat him to it.

15. Ignoring the chiropractor's reputation for being rough, Mr. Granger paid him a visit; by the time he left the office, he'd signed one check and two confessions.

16. But Mrs. Granger got revenge for the family. She also visited the chiropractor and made a point of asking if he'd treat her.
   "Naturally," he replied, so she left without paying.

17. "Doctor!" whined the patient, "I keep seeing spots before my eyes."

The physician scratched his head. "Why have you come to me? Have you seen an opthalmologist?"

"No," replied the patient, "just spots."

18. Then there was the egocentric ladies' man Dr. Goodstone. Whenever he took the pulse of one of his female patients, he routinely subtracted twenty beats per minute.

19. "He's a family doctor," Simpson told a friend. "He treats mine and I support his."

20. Then there was the patient whose doctor told him he had three months to live. When the patient informed him that he couldn't afford to pay the bill, the physician gave him another three months.

21. "I'm afraid," said the heart surgeon, "that you're going to need a bypass operation."

The patient squirmed uneasily in the seat. "I—I'd like a second opinion, if you don't mind."

"Not at all," replied the surgeon. "You're also ugly as sin."

22. The small-town newspaper sent a reporter to interview the new doctor in town.

"And what," she asked, "is your favorite recreation?"

"Actually," he smiled, "it's sleighing."

"No," she said, "I mean outside your profession."

23. It was just after midnight, and there was a rapping at the doctor's door. Dragging himself out of bed and poking his head from the window, he shouted down at the lone figure.

"Well?"

The woman looked up. "No, sick."

24. "Doc!" cried the caller, "my arm got broke in two places! What should I do?"

The sleepy GP replied, "Don't go back to either of them."

DOGS

See ANIMALS, CATS, PETS, and BLINDNESS 8, BUTCHERS 2, CLERGY 12, CLOTHING 2, SWIMMING 2

1. While sitting in the classroom waiting to take an exam, one veterinary student suddenly turned to another. "Good Lord," he declared, "I've just realized I haven't the faintest notion why dogs lick their balls!"

His colleague looked up. "Because they can."

2. Two young gays were strolling down a country road when they saw a dog off to one side, licking his genitals. Sighing, one of the young men said, "God, don't you wish you could do that?"

Licking his lips, the other said, "Yeah. Do you think he'd let me?"

3. Mr. Wells liked his dog's philosophy of life: If you can't eat it or screw it, piss on it.

4. Q: Why does a dog lift its leg to urinate?
   A: If it didn't shift gears, it'd crap on its paws.

5. Then there was the dog who jumped up and began licking the belly of his nymphomaniac owner, only to be admonished, "Down, boy!"

6. Despite such perks, that dog's favorite time of year was Christmas. It was a brief period when at long last the house had indoor plumbing.

7. When the dog gnawed a sizable hole in the new carpet, Mr. Alonzo went to call the dog-catcher.

His son Donald began wailing hysterically. "I'll train him, pop, I promise!"

"It's too late for that," his father snapped.

"No, it's not. I'll teach him to lie on the hole, and he *won't move!*"

8. Renfrew was the most absentminded altar boy

Father O'Malley had ever seen. But Renfrew meant well, and the clergymen decided to give him one more chance to prove himself.

"At mass tomorrow, I will come to a point where you'll hear me sing, 'And God's angels lit the candles.' When I say that, you're to light the candles in the back of the church. Is that understood?"

Renfrew said it was, and that night both the priest and Renfrew prayed for his success.

The next day Father O'Malley conducted mass in front of a full congregation. At last his rich baritone sang out, "And God's angels lit the candles!"

Nothing happened and he said again, "And God's angels lit the candles!"

Still the candles remained unlit, and once more he boomed, "And God's angels lit the candles!"

From behind the last pew Renfrew's small voice carried across the room. "And your dog pissed on the matches!"

9. Mr. Beemish went to the movie theater showing a revival of the old British comedy *The Mouse That Roared*. After the picture began, he became aware of an odd laugh several rows back. Turning, he noticed a sheepdog sitting beside his owner and laughing hysterically. Within moments the dog was in the aisle, convulsed with laughter, Mr. Beemish ambled over to the owner.

"Say, I just can't believe your dog here!"

"Neither can I," said the owner. "He loathed the book."

10. Epstein walked into the bar with his collie Jacob. Ordering a beer while Jacob sat at his feet, Epstein said to the bartender. "Say, I'll bet you a fin that my dog can talk."

Glancing down at the collie, the bartender pulled a five-dollar bill from his pocket and slapped it on the counter. "You're on."

Turning to the dog, Epstein said, "What's another way of saying fifty percent?"

The dog replied, "Arf!"

Scratching his head, the bartender pulled another bill from his pocket and lay it on the table. "Five bucks more says he can't answer another question."

Accepting the challenge, Epstein said, "What's the opposite of 'on'?"

"The dog replied. "Arf."

Catching on, the bartender said, "Okay, wise guy. Fifty bucks says he can't do it again . . . only this time *I'll* ask the question." Before Epstein could reply, the bartender had taken the money from the cash register and bent over to address the dog.

"Who's the greatest quarterback that ever played in the NFL?"

The dog replied, "Unitas?"

11. Mr. Maynard asked, "Got anything to cure fleas on a dog?"

    "That depends," the slow-minded vet replied. "What's wrong with them?"

12. The teacher asked his class, "If a dog is happy, it wags its tail. What does a goose do?"

    Little Vinnie blurt, "Piss the dog off?"

13. The dog walked into the Dodge City saloon and ordered a beer. Laughing, the bartender reached for his rifle, shot the dog in the foot, and snarled, "Scram! We don't serve dogs here!"

    A week later, the dog came back wearing his six-guns. Striding up to the new man at the bar, he said, "I'm looking for the man who shot my paw. . . ."

DOMESTICS

1. "On occasion," said Mrs. Fonebone to the new maid, "it will be necessary for you to help Mr. Fonebone's valet upstairs."

    "Of course, ma'am," replied the young domestic. "I've worked with lushes before."

2. Impressed with the porter on the overnight train, the millionaire offered him a job as his butler. The porter leaped at the opportunity.

Coming home from his office the first night of the butler's employ, the millionaire asked his wife how he'd worked out.

"Fine," she said hesitantly, then added, "except for one thing. He refuses to flush the toilet when the house is standing still."

DREAMS

1. Two men were sitting at a bar recounting their dreams.

"I dreamed I was on vacation," one man said fondly. "It was just me and my fishing rod and this big beautiful lake. What a dream."

"I had a great dream too," said the other. "I dreamed I was in bed with two beautiful women and having the time of my life."

His companion looked over and exhorted, "You dreamed you had two women, and you didn't call me?"

"Oh, I did," said the other, "but when I called, your wife said you'd gone fishing."

2. "Doc," said the young man lying down on the couch, "you've *got* to help me! Every night I have the same horrible dream. I'm lying in bed when all of a sudden five women rush in and start tearing off my clothes."

The psychiatrist nodded. "And what do *you* do?"

"I push them away."

"I see. What do you want *me* to do?"

The patient implored. "Break my arms."

3. The woman rolled over in bed, a big smile on her face. "Oh, Jules," she sighed, "I just dreamed that you were such an angel and bought me a fur coat."

Recognizing a trap when he saw one, Jules replied, "In your next dream, wear it in good health."

DRINKING   *See* BEER and ANIMALS 4,
COLLEGE 4, FUNDRAISERS 1, HOMOSEXUALS 8,
HOTELS 1, MARRIAGE 20, PRESIDENTS 6,
SAILING 1, SINGLES 2, TRAINS 1,
WRESTLING 1

1. Perhaps the most notorious drunk of all was the one who saw the billboard that read, "Drink Canada Dry." He went there and did.

2. Returning to his hotel room after a few too many, the drunk executive walked into the elevator shaft and promptly dropped five stories. Lying bloodied and broken and flat on his back, he stared back along the shaft and sneered, "I wanted to go *up*, dammit!"

3. Then there was the vice-president who drank to the health of so many of his clients that he lost his own.

4. Which wasn't as unusual as the drunk who felt ill, so he mixed orange juice with milk of magnesia and made a Phillips screwdriver.

5. And let's not overlook the *bon vivant* who had a bit too much wine with dinner and the next morning suffered the wrath of grapes. . . .

6. The millionaire was concerned when liquor started vanishing from the mansion shortly after he hired a new butler.

   Confronted with his employer's suspicions, the butler said, "I'll have you know I come from a long line of honest Englishmen."

   Smelling alcohol on the butler's breath, the millionaire said, "To be very frank, it's not your English forebears which concerns me but your Scotch extraction."

7. Sitting beside Ben in the bar was the ugliest woman he'd ever laid eyes on; so ugly was she, in fact, that he refused each and every one of her advances.

   After a while, having had one too many, the woman said, "Y'know, mishter, if I have one more drink I'm really gonna feel it."

Turning to the woman, Ben said, "T'tell the truth, sister, if I have one more drink, I prob'ly won't mind."

8. For years Dr. Benson had left his office and gone to Teddy's Bar, where Teddy would fix him a daiquiri laced with crushed pecans. One day, however, Teddy ran out of pecans; instead, he substituted hickory nuts.

Dr. Benson sat down and took a sip under Teddy's watchful eyes; he frowned.

"Say, Teddy, this isn't an almond daiquiri. Just what *is* it?"

"I can't lie to ya," Teddy said. "It's a hickory daiquiri, Doc."

9. The couple was dining out when the wife noticed a familiar face at the bar.

"Elliot," she said, pointing, "do you see that man downing bourbon at the bar?" The husband looked over and nodded. "Well," the woman continued, "he's been drinking like that for ten years, ever since I jilted him."

The husband returned to his meal. "Nonsense," he said, "even that's not worth so much celebrating."

DRUGS

1. Then there was the mother who stumbled upon her daughter getting high and, tearing the marijuana cigarette from her mouth, yelled, "What's a joint like this doing in a nice girl like you?"

DRUGGISTS   See FOOD 7

1. The druggist approached the customer who had just lit a cigar. "Excuse me," he said, "but you can't smoke in here."

   The irate patron puffed a stream of smoke from the side of his mouth. "Like hell I can't! I just bought the damn thing here!"

   "Big deal!" replied the druggist. "We sell condoms here too!"

2. Then there was the moron who went to the drugstore to buy deodorant.

   "The ball type?" asked the clerk.

   "No," replied the moron, "the kind that goes under the arms."

3. Concerned about her husband's impotence but aware that he would never admit it was a prob-

lem, Mrs. Franklin went to the family doctor, who prescribed something to cure it. Stopping off at the pharmacy, she had the prescription filled; unfortunately, the druggist misread the doctor's writing and instead of typing "4 Teaspoons" on the label, he listed the dosage as "40 Teaspoons."

The following day, Mrs. Franklin burst into her doctor's office.

"What's wrong?" he asked as he faced the frantic woman. "Didn't the medicine work?"

"Did it ever!" she replied. "Now I need the antidote so they can shut the coffin!"

4. The patron staggered to the counter, wincing. "Say, would you give me something for my head?"

The pharmacist looked up. "Why? What would *I* do with it?"

5. Mr. Wells ran up to the counter and began screaming at the pharmacist. "You idiot! When I brought my wife's prescription in before, you filled it with strychnine instead of quinine!"

"I see," the druggist replied. "That will cost you five dollars more."

6. Mr. Ettinger went to the drugstore to purchase an aphrodisiac. Explaining that he had two young ladies coming to visit that night, Mr. Ettinger was delighted when the pharmacist gave him the most powerful love stimulant on the market.

"Make sure, though, that you take it at least two hours beforehand, since it has to be assimilated totally into the bloodstream."

Mr. Ettinger did as he was told and the following morning he returned to the drugstore. Walking over to the counter, he said, "What have you got to soothe raw flesh?"

The pharmacist winked knowingly. "Your penis, sir?"

"No," he replied, "my hand. The girls didn't show."

DWARFS   *See* PERSONALS 1

1. The dwarf didn't really want to make love to the Amazon, but someone put him up to it.

2. Then there was the woman who heard that dwarfs were superb lovers and said to one, "Give me nine inches and make it hurt!" So he screwed her three times and punched her.

3. Q: What do you call a gay dwarf?
   A: A low blow.

4. Furious at finding her husband in bed with a female dwarf, the long-suffering wife screamed, "I thought you said you'd never cheat on me again."

"So I did," he said defensively, "I'm tapering off."

5. Then there was the basketball player whose most devoted fan was a lady dwarf. He was nuts over her, too.

EGGS

1. The farm boy said to his father, "Y'know, pop, I've just realized that an egg is the unluckiest danged thing in all creation."

   "And why is that?" asked the elder farmer.

   "'Cuz," replied the boy, "it only gets laid once, it only gets eaten once, it takes eleven minutes to get hard, it comes in a box with eleven other guys, and the only one who ever sits on its face is its mom. . . ."

ELEPHANTS   See CIRCUS 5

1. Q: What do elephants use for vibrators?
   A: Epileptics.

2. "Now, class," said Mrs. Ackerman, "would someone please tell me where elephants are found?"

   "Gee," squealed little Roderick, "I thought they were so big they never got lost!"

3. Q: Why can't two elephants go swimming at the same time?
   A: Because they only have one pair of trunks.

4. Q: What did the grape say when the elephant stepped on it?
   A: Nothing. it just let out a little wine.

5. Q: What do you give an elephant with diarrhea?
   A: Plenty of room.

6. Q: What did Hannibal get when he crossed the Alps with elephants?
   A: Mountains that never forget.

ELEVATORS

1. When the elevator stalled, the couple trapped inside decided to get off between floors.

ENGAGEMENTS   *See* MARRIAGE

1. When he gave her a diamond heart-shaped pendant for Valentine's Day, the young man's fiancée said, "Darling, please—I don't want to wait until we're married to make love. Let's do it now."

But her virtuous lover replied, "We *must* wait. It won't be long until May."

Cocking a brow, the woman said, "Really? And how long will it be *then*?"

2. Then there was the pundit who figured out that showers are only thrown for women because their fiancés are already washed up. . . .

THE ENVIRONMENT

1. You know that pollution is bad when the leaves don't fall, they jump.

2. Then there were the good old days, when you went on a picnic and the black spots on your food were grains of pepper.

3. But things will get better. The EPA promises to do something about pollution as soon as they can see their way clear.

4. Then there was the anti-environmentalist who pointed out that over 200 million trees had been cut down in the campaign to warn us about squandering our natural resources.

5. Two killer whales watched helplessly as a Jap-

anese fishing boat hauled in a net filled with tuna . . . and two stray dolphins.

Shaking its head, one killer whale said to the other, "Look who's calling names."

6. Then there was the well-meaning citizen who hired a plane and flew across the countryside dropping thousands of leaflets. They proclaimed, "A cleaner environment is up to you."

7. Then there was the scholar who pointed out that water pollution is so bad it takes more courage to be a Baptist than a marine. . . .

8. Proof of the sorry state of the water is that when the dam collapsed the water didn't.

EPILEPTICS
See DISEASES, LEPERS
and ELEPHANTS 1

1. Q: What do you call an epileptic in a vegetable garden?
A: A seizure salad.

2. Q: What's the difference between an epileptic corn farmer and a prostitute with diarrhea?
A: One shucks between fits. . . .

3. The powerful Burmese Shan warrior went to

his doctor complaining of terrible seizures. Unfortunately, the physician wasn't schooled in these matters and sent for a specialist, Dr. Lao.

"I can only help you," said Lao, "if I'm there when a seizure occurs. To cure you, I'll have to live with you."

Agreeing to take the specialist in, the Shan made room for him in his spacious tent. For weeks the two men were inseparable. Finally, however, the Shan had to join his tribesmen in battle—and demanded that the specialist go with him.

As it happened, the warrior had a seizure on the battlefield, and, running to his side, the specialist was killed in a hail of arrows. The moral of the story: Hang back when the fit hits the Shan.

ESKIMOS

1. Upon making his way to the fringes of the Arctic Circle, the great nineteenth-century explorer Randolph Wood met a group of Eskimo men who, out on an extended hunt, invited him to spend a night at their igloo.

As they sat around the ice hut eating fish, the Eskimos invited the brave explorer to become a member of their tribe.

"To do so," the leader explained, "you must

drink five cupfuls of our potent brew Shlur, wrestle a polar bear, and rape a woman from the hated Hanoki tribe."

Anxious to reach this pinnacle of achievement, Randolph agreed to the challenge. Guzzling down the Shlur, which was served in the skull of a walrus, he then asked where to find a polar bear and set out to accomplish his first task.

Several hours passed, and the Eskimo hunters began to fear that he had perished in pursuit of his goal. Finally, however, Wood staggered into the igloo. He was bloodied, his clothes shredded, but on his face was a look that was pure triumph.

"Well," he boasted, "I did it! I finished the first two parts of my task. Now just tell me where to find that woman you want me to wrestle."

2. Then there was the Eskimo lesbian who was fond of cold cuts. . . .

EXTRATERRESTRIALS

1. When his spaceship was struck by a meteor, the alien was forced to land on Earth. Walking around, he approached Hymie's Deli and saw bagels in the window; smiling, he hurried inside.

"Sir," he said in halting English, "I wonder if I might buy two wheels for my spacecraft."

Hymie had no idea what the extraterrestrial was talking about until he pointed a spindly green finger at the bagels in the window.

"Oh, no . . . no," grinned Hymie, "those aren't wheels . . . those are bagels."

Not certain that he'd made himself clear, "Sir, I would like to buy two of those wheels for my spacecraft."

Hymie's good humor began to waver. "Lissen, greenie, I said those are *bagels*. They're for eating."

Still smiling, the alien said, "Sir, I would like to buy two of those wheels for my spacecraft."

Getting angry now, Hymie turned and pulled a bagel from the bin, handed it to the alien, and told him to taste it. So doing, the little green man looked at Hymie and nodded.

"You know," he said, "this would go great with cream cheese."

2. Stopping at the theatre where a reissue of *Frankenstein* was playing, the extraterrestrial stared long and hard at the poster. Finally a companion came along to find out what was keeping him. Seeing the picture of the monster, the newcomer yelled, "Sex! Is that all you ever think about?"

3. The president was awakened late one night by an urgent call from the Pentagon.

"Mr. President," said the four-star general, barely able to contain himself, "there's good news and bad news."

"Oh no," muttered the president. "Well, let me have the bad news first."

"The bad news, sir, is that we've been invaded by creatures from another planet."

"Christ, and the good news?"

"The good news, sir, is that they eat reporters and piss oil."

4. During their first visit to earth, the two glowing Martians stood on a streetcorner staring at a traffic light. Suddenly it went from green to red. Turning to his companion, one Martian said disgustedly, "Let's get out of here. If there's one thing I hate it's a woman who's a tease."

5. The two Uranians land in the desert, and, leaving their saucer hidden beneath a dune, they go exploring. The first sign of civilization they spot is a service station and, approaching warily, Commander Znugg says to science officer Ktoing, "Watch it, this is gonna be rough."

"How do you know?" asked Ktoing.

"Trust me," Znugg replied as they walked up to the nearest gas pump. Trying to sound as pleasant as possible, Znugg said, "Take me to your leader."

The pump stood there impassively, and Znugg repeated her demand. Once again the pump made no response, and, growing intemperate, Znugg unholstered her firearm. When the pump refused to answer for a third time, she shot a single firebolt into the machine, and the resultant explosion blew the explorers from Uranus all the way back to their saucer. Rising unsteadily to his feet, Ktoing helped Znugg to hers.

"Bstoz my ptooties!" he exclaimed. "How did you know the earthling would be so intransigent?"

Brushing herself off, Znugg replied, "Anyone who has a dick so long they can stick it in their ear has to be one tough cookie!"

FAME

1. Disc jockey Alfonse Alfonso was riding the bus to work and his chest swelled when he heard a mother say to her young son, "Teddy, do you want to listen to the *Alfonse Alfonso Show* when we get home?"

"No!" snapped the child.

"Then behave yourself."

1. Lying in bed with his wife, the farmer stroked
her bare breasts and said, "Y'know, Maybelle, if
these gave milk we could sell the cow."

   Sighing, Maybelle lay her hand on her husband's crotch. "And if this stayed hard just a
little longer, we could fire the farmhand."

2. Needing to double his output of eggs, the farmer
went to his neighbor and asked if he could buy a
few of his roosters.

   "Ya'll only need this'n," said the farmer, handing him a handsome red bird. Dubious, the
farmer paid for the rooster and went home.

   The next morning he went to the barn and
found feathers all over the place: Every chicken
looked whipped, and he learned that his rooster
had screwed every one of them.

   "Yer gonna screw yerself t'death!" the farmer
warned, and went about his chores.

   The next morning he went back to the barn
and found that this time the bird had not only
screwed all the chickens but the sheep as well.

   "I'm tellin' ya, yer gonna screw yerself t'death,"
he repeated, and went about his chores.

   The next morning he went to the barn and

found that not only the chickens and sheep had been screwed, but the cows, horses, and family dog as well. Noticing that the rooster wasn't around, the farmer went back outside and found him lying face down in the field. Standing over the prone bird, he says, "Didn't I warn ya? Didn't I say ya'd screw yerself to death?"

Suddenly one of the bird's eyes opened. "Will you shut up!" he demanded. "You want to scare away the buzzards?"

3. Mr. Greenjeans said to Mr. Bluejeans, "Me? I like to wake up with the rooster. How about you?"

Mr. Bluejeans shook his head. "Naw, I prefer sleeping in my own bed."

4. "Now son," the farmer said to the new farmhand, "are you sure you know just how long cows should be milked?"

"Sure," said the hired help. "Just the same as short ones."

5. Then there was the slow-witted farmer who took his sick chicken to the vet and asked what he should do.

"Make chicken soup," the vet said glumly.

Returning home, the hopeful farmer promptly killed a chicken and fed some to the sick bird.

6. Then there was the farmer who didn't realize

he was growing crops on a former nuclear test site. Everyone who ate his produce came down with atomic ache. . . .

7. Q: What goes peck, peck, peck, boom?
    A: A chicken in a minefield.

FAT   *See* DIETS and SUICIDE 1

1. "It was terrible," the man told his friend the day after a blind date. "Her measurements were 36-24-36."
    "Terrible?" exclaimed the friend, "I can't understand why you're complaining!"
    "Because her other leg was the same!"

2. Q: How do you make love to a fat woman?
    A: Roll her in flour and go for the wet spot.

3. The fat young woman said to her psychiatrist, "Doctor, I just don't know what to do. My boyfriend can't keep his eyes off other women."
    As discreetly as possible, the doctor said, "Marianne, why don't you diet?"
    The woman brightened. "Hey . . . that's a good idea. What color?"

4. Gary and Harry watched as portly Mrs. Chester climbed onto the scale and plugged a penny

in the slot. The scale stopped at thirty-eight pounds, and, unaware that it was broken, Gary gasped, "My God, she's hollow!"

THE FBI

1. The most ineffective G-man of the year has to be the FBI agent who was told to keep tabs on the leader of the Gay Militant League and blew the assignment.

FEMINISM

1. It didn't take long for the feminists in the office to get up in arms about the notice posted in the executive lounge: "Any vice-president whose secretary is ill or on vacation may take advantage of the girls who work the reception desk."

2. Then there was the leading feminist who, before she realized what she was saying, decried anti-ERA women by telling an interviewer, "As long as women are split like we are, men will remain on top."

3. Sick and tired of their history professor's lewd jokes and sexual innuendo, a group of girls de-

cided that the next time he uttered an inappropriate remark they would get up and leave in protest. However, overhearing their plan and looking to score some points with the teacher, a fellow student informed him of their scheme.

The next day, after chatting about current events for a few minutes, the teacher suddenly smiled and, making a clever segue, said, "You know, I hear there's a shortage of whores in Paris—"

Exchanging resolute looks, the girls rose as one and started to leave the room. Following them with innocent eyes, the professor said, "Girls, where are you going? The next plane doesn't leave until tonight."

4. Then there are those who complain that feminism has gone too far with the Boston Pops and Moms Orchestra . . .

5. . . . and the cereal that goes snap, mom, and pop.

FINANCE

1. Mr. DeBois knew the American dollar was low, but he didn't know just *how* low until he was in Rome, threw three coins in the fountain, and was arrested—for littering.

2. Upon returning home, Mr. DeBois spread the word, complaining to his friends that dollars to donuts was finally an even bet.

3. Hal met Robert at the diner.

"Would you believe I just burned a thousand-dollar bill?"

"Jeez," said Robert, "I envy your success."

"What success? It was easier to burn it than to pay it."

4. Later that day Hal and Robert met in the street.

"Why are you walking?" asked Hal.

"To save a buck."

Hal thought for a moment, then suggested, "Why not take the long way and save two bucks?"

FIRE FIGHTERS   *See* FOOTBALL 3

1. The call came into the firehouse just as the crew had sat down to dinner.

"Quick!" said the caller, "you've got to come to 10 Cherry Lane! There's a fire in my basement!"

"Did you try throwing water on it?" inquired the fire fighter.

"Of course I did!"

The fire fighter replied, "Then there's no reason for us to come. That's all *we* do."

2. John met his old friend David in the street, and after a moment David inquired about the wife of his acquaintance.

"I'm afraid," John said, "that I lost my wife in a fire."

David's features clouded over. "I'm sorry. How did it happen?"

"Well, we were eating lamb flambé when the plate overturned on her dress."

"My God," said David, "you mean she burned to death?"

"No. The fire fighters arrived in time and she drowned."

3. The phone rang at the fire station.

"Hurry!" said the panicked voice, "we've got a big fire at the store!"

"How do we get there?" the fire fighter demanded.

"Dammit," shouted the caller. "Use the big red truck!"

FISHING   *See* THE ENVIRONMENT 5

1. "Excuse me," said the game warden approaching the hillbilly, "but you need a permit in order to fish here."

The moron glanced at his full basket of fish. "Why? I'm doin' just fine with a worm."

2. Gizelle said to her neighbor, "Don't tell me you believe your husband's story that he spent the day fishing. Why, he didn't come home with a single fish."

"That's why I believe him," the neighbor noted.

3. "There are two types of fishermen," Roddy told his nephew as he cast his line. "Those who fish for sport, and those who catch something."

4. Beau tied his boat to the dock where his wife was waiting. He hadn't landed a thing, so he put a few creative touches on the one fish he had managed to hook.

"You should have seen the one that got away," he embellished. "We fought for over an hour out there, and . . . I swear, Dolly, that beast was a hundred pounds if he was an ounce."

Looking over her sunglasses, Dolly replied, "Beau, one of the other wives loaned me her binoculars. That fish would have fit in our home aquarium."

Undaunted, Beau said, "You must've been watching at the end. Amazing how much weight those suckers can lose in an hour."

1. "My husband's always playing around," Liz complained to Debbie as they pedaled their exercise bicycles one morning. "It's made me so anxious I can't even eat."

"Then why don't you leave him?" Debbie asked.

"Oh, I will," replied Liz, "just as soon as I hit 105."

2. Mr. Goodman was walking down the street when he passed a fitness center with a sign outside which read, "Lose five pounds in five minutes: $25."

Curious, Mr. Goodman went inside, paid his money, and was shown to a gymnasium. After a few minutes a young girl entered. She was naked except for a small sign around her waist: "If you catch me, this is yours." On the bottom of the sign was an arrow pointing down.

Rubbing his hands together, Mr. Goodman gave chase. However, after five minutes of frantic chasing he wasn't able to catch her. Stepping on the scale, he was delighted to see that he was, however, five pounds lighter.

Leaving the fitness center, Mr. Goodman walked further along the street when he saw another fitness center with an even more enticing sign: it read, "Lose ten pounds in five minutes: $50.'

Curious to see how he could double his weight loss, Mr. Goodman went in and paid his fee. As before, he was shown to a gym. This time, however, he was greeted by a hulking brute of a man who was also naked and, like the girl, wore a sign about his waist. Only this one read, "If I catch you, you get *this*!"

FLATULENCE *See* CONSTIPATION and MORONS 15

1. Each and every time he broke wind, the word *honda* would flutter from the man's behind. Going to the doctor, he demonstrated this phenomenon —which, much to his surprise, didn't faze the doctor in the least.

   Going round to the man's mouth, the physician found an abscessed tooth, which he promptly pulled. At once the man's problem was solved.

   "That's amazing!" said the patient. "But tell me, how did you know what to do?"

   "Simple," answered the doctor. "Everyone knows that abscess makes the fart go 'honda.' "

2. Mr. Youngman was brought to the lounge of the nursing home to await his son. Since he was especially frail, the nurse was never far from his side.

As it happened, at least once every minute the ninety-year-old would tilt slightly to one side; as soon as he did so, the nurse hurried over and straightened him right up.

Finally Mr. Youngman's son Bob arrived.

"Well, pop," he said, "how're they treating you here?"

He replied, "The food's fine and the accomodations are even better—but there *is* one thing."

"What's that?"

Cocking his eyes over his shoulder, he said, "It's that sonofabitchin' nurse over there. He won't let me fart!"

3. Q: Why do women break wind after they urinate?
   A: They can't shake it, so they blow-dry it.

4. Q: Why do farts smell?
   A: So deaf people can enjoy them, too.

5. While she was awaiting for the members of her bridge club to arrive, Mrs. Finster accidentally loosed a whopper of a fart. The scent was unmistakable, and, fishing out a can of air freshener, she hurriedly sprayed the room.

   Mrs. Jackson arrived minutes later and, sniffing the air as she walked in the front door, she candidly announced, "Christ, Lizzie! It smells like someone shit in a pine tree!"

6. Norman came in from the field one day and found his mother carefully spreading handful after handful of manure over the watermelon patch.

"Maw," he said, "there's an easier way of doin' that."

So saying, he took a stick of dynamite and, lighting it, tossed it under the outhouse. However, Norman didn't know his great-grandmother was using the facility just then, and when the TNT ignited, it vaporized the outhouse and blew the woman nearly a mile into the air. She landed, with a considerable thud, in the midst of the watermelons.

"Good Lawd," Norman yelled, "are y'all right, great grannie?"

The feisty old woman rose unsteadily. "I reckon I am," she replied. "All I kin say is I'm glad I didn't let *that* one go in the house!"

7. Then there was the considerate housewife who served her family beans with curry because she liked Indian music.

8. Q: What's invisible and smells like carrots?
   A: Rabbit farts.

FLOWER CHILDREN

1. Reminiscing about their wayward youth, a former hippie asked a onetime flower child, "Say, were you ever picked up by the fuzz?"

   "No," she replied, "but I bet it'd hurt."

FLOWERS

See GARDENING

1. Wishing to prove to his wife that he loved her for more than sex, the young man bought her a lovely bouquet of roses. Despite his good intentions, however, the devoted husband received a suspicious look when he handed her the flowers.

   "I suppose," she said, "that now you expect me to spend the weekend on my back with my legs spread."

   "Why?" said the young man. "Don't we have a vase?"

2. After an all-night party a hung over young gay is feeling very sore in the posterior. Going to his proctologist, he's surprised when the doctor announces, "Young man, did you know that you have a dozen roses up here?"

   Turning excitedly, the gay cried, "Oooh . . . read the card! Read the card!"

3. Due to a mixup at the flower shop, it was the bookseller moving to larger quarters who received the wreath with the card saying, "With sympathy," and the family of the late Mr. Miller who received the flowers which read, "Best of luck in your new location."

FOOD

See COOKING, PIZZA, RESTAURANTS, and BUSINESS 1, EXTRATERRESTRIALS 1, FARMERS 6, FLATULENCE 7, GEOGRAPHY 1, HILLBILLIES 6, INFLATION 4, KIDS 8, WORMS 2

1. Q: Why did the fig go out with a prune?
   A: It couldn't find another date.

2. Q: Why do watermelons contains so much water?
   A: They're planted in the spring.

3. Q: What side of a peach is the left one?
   A: The uneaten side.

4. "Doctor," said Mrs. Grell, "are bran flakes really healthy?"
   "Well," replied the dim-witted physician, "I've never had to treat one."

5. Then there was the efficiency expert who put Visine in his grapefruit. . . .

6. And the shopper who stopped buying Kool-Aid because she couldn't figure out how to get two quarts of water into the envelope.

7. The pharmacist proudly showed Mr. Thompson his newest product. "It's an apple that tastes like pussy."

   Curious, Mr. Thompson took a bite; he spat violently. "Pussy? This thing tastes like shit!"

   The pharmacist flushed and turned it around. "Sorry," he said, "you bit the wrong side."

8. Ida confided to her close friend, "My cooking left my husband cold."

   "He divorced you?"

   "No," she replied, "he died."

FOOTBALL   *See* BASEBALL, BOXING, GOLF, HOCKEY, SOCCER, WRESTLING, and DOGS 10

1. Football is a game in which a handful of men run around for two hours watched by millions of people who could really use the exercise.

2. The football player swaggered into the crowded bar, where the only available stool was next to a floral-scented gay man. The halfback scowled as he sat down.

"Your kind make me sick," he muttered under his breath. "You're limp-wristed little shits, all of you."

Growing indignant, the gay man said, "Nonsense! Why, I'll bet I can beat you at a game of bar football."

"Bar football?" the halfback snorted. "What's that?"

Rather than explain, the gay ordered a beer and chugged it down without pausing for breath. "Touchdown!" he cheered, then stood, dropped his pants, and farted. "Extra point!" he exclaimed.

"Shit," said the halfback, "you don't stand a chance."

Ordering a beer, he gulped it down and stood, dropping his pants. However, before he could break wind, the gay had plugged the halfback's ass with his own rigid member.

"Blocked kick!" he shouted, "I win!"

3. The wide receiver was walking down the street, mulling over what he had done right and wrong in the team scrimmage, when he heard fire engines in the distance. Looking down the street, he saw that they were racing toward a burning building. He noticed flames in the top floor and a woman on the ledge; in her arms was an infant.

Running over, he shouted, "Lady, throw me the kid!"

"No!" she screamed, "it's five stories down!"

"Don't worry, I'm a professional football player. I promise I'll catch it!"

Reluctantly the woman tightened the baby's blanket, leaned over, and released the child. The wide receiver watched it carefully, moving to the left and right as the winds nudged the baby this way or that. He was moving, constantly moving, dancing on the tips of his toes; his arms were extended, bent slightly at the elbows to give slightly with the impact, fingers wriggling in anticipation.

Fourth floor, third floor, second . . . the baby spun end over end, then caught a sudden thermal draft and swung several yards out toward the street. Jumping in that direction, the wide receiver lunged and stretched his fingers, barely catching the child. He bobbled it for a second, carried across the street by his own momentum, nearly dropping it; then he pulled it in and hugged it to his chest just as he crossed the curb on the other side of the street.

Retaining his footing, he let out a cheer and spiked the baby.

4. The highly competitive running back went to the team medic.

"You have a flu," said the doctor as he looked down at the thermometer, "and unless this fever goes down, you won't be playing Sunday."

"How high is it?" the athlete inquired.

"Just over a hundred degrees."

The running back considered this, then said, "What's the team record?"

5. Tired of hearing about how dumb football players were, college coach Grabowski remembered a recent press release that crossed his desk and told the television interviewer, "It so happens that according to a recent Harrison Poll, over fifty percent of the young men who play college football are making straight A's."

"I read that report, too," the interviewer replied, "and my question is this: When will they learn to write the rest of the alphabet?"

6. The dean and the coach struck a simple deal: Despite his abysmal grades, the all-star tackle could play in the big game if and only if he could learn and remember the formula for water before then.

The coach and the chemistry teacher both worked with the gridiron star and were confident that he'd come through with flying colors.

On the morning of the game the dean came down to the locker where the tackle was suiting up.

"Well?" said the dean. "What is the formula for water?"

Grinning broadly, and drawing confidence from the presence of his proud coach, the player said, "H-I-J-K-L-M-N-O."

FORTUNE-TELLERS

1. Visiting the carnival midway, Doug noticed the fortune-teller's tent and popped inside. The room was done in somber purples, with a dull white glow coming from an ancient crystal ball. An old gypsy woman was bent over the orb, and she looked up when Doug entered.

   "Hi," he said in response to her stony gaze. "I'd like my fortune told."

   Nodding, the woman said gravely, "I will answer two of your questions for one hundred dollars."

   "One hundred dollars!" Doug balked. "Isn't that terribly expensive for this kind of service?"

   "Yes it is," she replied, "And what is your second question?"

FOUL LANGUAGE

1. After overhearing her young son use a four-letter word, Mrs. Flaherty ran into his room.

   "Jason!" she roared, "I don't ever want to hear that kind of language again!"

   "But mom," he said defensively, "J. D. Salinger uses it!"

She shot back, "Then you're not to play with him ever again!"

FUNDRAISERS

See RAFFLES

1. Jack was the most successful fundraiser in town. Not only did he stagger people at the sums he collected, but he confused them as well: No one could understand why the checks were always signed with swizzle sticks.

GALLEY SLAVES

1. The galley officer rose when the commander entered the galley. The two men exchanged words, after which the Roman officer left.

   Standing behind his drums, the officer said, "I have good news and I have bad news," he said. "The good news is that we won't, in fact, be going into battle with the Macedonian pirates. The bad news," he went on, "is that Commmander Arrius wishes to go water-skiing."

GAMBLING *See* CARD GAMES and ACCENTS 2,
DOGS 10, HORSES 1,
LIBRARIANS 1, WRESTLING 1

1. Jack loved watching the races on the TV at the bar, but he wasn't the brightest guy on earth: betting with one patron, he lost twenty dollars on a race and then lost another sawbuck on the instant replay.

2. After years of gambling, Maxie finally figured out how to win a small fortune in Las Vegas: He went with a large one.

3. Then there was the moron who went to the track for the first time and knew his horse was a shoo-in. His animal was listed as starting at fifteen to one while the race didn't start until one.

4. Murphy came home from a night of cards to find his wife sitting up, a cross expression on her face. "You said you'd be home by 11:45," she charged, "and here it is 3:00 A.M.! I've been worried sick about you."

   "But you misunderstood, darling," he sprung his trap, "I'm right on time! I told you I'd be home by a quarter of twelve . . . and I am."

GARDENING

See FLOWERS

1. Hector's thumb was anything but green. In fact, he was such an inept gardener that his wife dubbed the garden a Forest Lawn for seeds.

2. However, Hector did learn one thing from his experience. The first thing you do with a garden is turn the soil over . . . to a gardener.

GENE SPLICING

1. After crossing a parrot with a lion, the scientists weren't exactly sure what they had. But one fact was irrefutable: When it talked, people listened.

GENIES

See MUSIC 1

1. The young man was walking along the beach when an old lantern washed ashore. Picking it up and brushing off the sand, he was surprised when an ancient genie appeared in a puff of smoke. Said he:

I am the djinn of Timbuktu;
He that finds me has wishes two.

Amazed, the young man thought for a moment. "Two wishes, huh? What I wish is that I can always be hard and that I can get all the ass I want."

"As you wish," said the genie, and he promptly turned the young man into a toilet seat.

2. The young black man was poking around in an alley when, much to his surprise, he found a magic lamp. Rubbing it, he was delighted when a genie appeared and boldly announced:

I am the djinn of Timbuktu
He that finds me has wishes two.

Beside himself with glee, the youth says, "Genie, my first wish is to be uptight and outasight, and my second wish is to be inside a nice, warm pussy."

Bowing obeisantly, the genie turned the youth into a Tampax.

3. Lenny walked into his favorite bar one night, and, much to the bartender's surprise, he saw that Lenny's head had shrunk to roughly the size of a softball. For the first few rounds the bartender pretended not to notice, but at last his curiosity got the best of him.

"Say," he said, "I hate to ask, but isn't your head just a bit smaller than it was last night?"

Lenny nodded glumly, and the bartender asked

what had happened. "It's like this," Lenny said, "I was walking along the beach when all of a sudden a bottle washed up on shore. As I picked it up, it happened to brush my sleeve; all of a sudden there's a cloud of smoke and out steps a genie. I tell ya, she was the most beautiful woman I've ever seen. So when she says she'll grant me one wish, the first thing I ask is to go to bed with her. 'I'm sorry,' she says, 'but it's against the genie law to do that.' So I said, 'Well then, how about a little head. . . .' "

4. The Briton, the Canadian, and the hillbilly were all washed ashore on an uncharted island. The only food and drink came from coconuts, and after several days they began to despair.

One morning, however, a lantern washed ashore, and the Briton picked it up. More despairing than hopeful, he rubbed it: Out came a genie, who promised to grant each of the men one wish.

His eyes wide with thanksgiving, the Briton said, "I wish I were back at my cottage in Ipswich!"

The genie snapped his fingers, and the Briton was gone.

The Canadian said, "I wish I were back at my home in Gananoque."

The genie snapped his fingers and the Canadian was gone.

Looking around, the hillbilly began to weep. "I—I'm so lonely," he wailed, "I wish the other two guys were back."

GEOGRAPHY

1. Q: What's purple and surrounded by water?
   A: Grape Britain.

2. Then there was the girl from Burma who went out to find a Mandalay.

GHETTOS   See GENIES 2

1. Q: What is foreplay in the ghetto?
   A: "Stay cool, bitch, I got a knife."

2. Then there was the ghetto school that was so badly underfunded that the only hot lunches were those that were stolen.

GHOSTS   See also DEATH

1. When their favorite waiter died, a few of the diner's regulars decided to try and contact him through a medium.

"In order to communicate with the dead," the medium advised those gathered around the table, "we must all hold hands and mutter his name as one."

Sitting at the round table, the group locked hands, and when the medium counted three, the men said quietly and reverently, "Moe Iskowitz."

There was nothing but silence, and after several minutes, they tried again. Once again the waiter failed to show. Finally, after the third "Moe Iskowitz," the bald-headed man appeared as a spectral image floating above them.

"Moe," said one of the men, "it's good to see you, but why did we have to call you three times?"

The ectoplasmic waiter shrugged. "Jerk, this isn't my table!"

GIGOLOS

See SEX

1. Q: How did the gigolo know he'd been sleep-walking?
   A: He woke up in his own bed.

2. Then there was the gigolo who succeeded in business thanks to his alert staff.

3. Unfortunately, he contracted leprosy and his business fell off.

See BASEBALL, BOXING, FOOTBALL, HOCKEY, SOCCER, WRESTLING and DIVORCE 1, TRAVEL 5, 9

1. A handsome young golfer was playing in his first professional tournament. At the end of the first day's activity, the novice was ahead, and a beautiful woman sidled up to him in the clubhouse.

"Say," she cooed, "do you swing as well off the green?"

Rising to the challenge, he took the girl back to his hotel room, and they made love, after which he rolled over and went to sleep.

"Hey," she shook him awake, "Tom Watson wouldn't give up so quickly!"

Mustering his energies, he made love to her a second time, after which he slipped off, quite exhausted.

The woman shook him again. "Hey, Arnold Palmer wouldn't give up so quickly!"

The golfer was getting some life back in his jaw, and, taking a deep breath, he made love to her yet again. When he was through, he fell asleep on top of her, too tired to move. She tapped him on the shoulder.

"Hey, Jack Nicklaus wouldn't fade away like that!"

Angry and just a touch mortified, the golfer rose. "Say—just what *is* par for this hole, anyway?"

2. While he was sitting on the sundeck of the golf club, Morty was hit in the head with a ball. By the time the offending golfer had chased down his shot, Morty had an ice pack on his head and was ripping mad.

"I'm going to take you to court!" he screamed at the golfer. "I'll sue you for five million dollars!"

Distressed, the golfer said feebly, "I said 'fore'—"

With a triumphant look, Morty announced, "I'll take it!"

3. Mr. Carter was playing golf, and no sooner had he teed off than the ball went wild and landed in the rough.

"Oh, shit!" he swore, then quickly looked skyward and said, "Forgive me, Lord, I won't do that again."

Playing the second hole, Mr. Carter missed an easy putt. "Oh, shit!" he roared, then glanced heavenward and hurriedly apologized again.

Moving onto the third hole, he made another awful shot into the rough. "Oh, shit!" he said yet again, then once again apologized.

As he moved on to the fourth hole, there was a thunderclap and a bolt of lightning struck Mr. Carter dead.

"Oh, shit!" boomed the loud voice from above.

4. Then there was the golfer whose game was so bad that the only time he broke a hundred was when he went grocery shopping. . . .

5. And the golfer whose sex life was terrible because of his unusually short putts.

6. Not to mention the farsighted golfer who drove his caddy's nuts. . . .

7. "It's true," the weekend golfer told his wife on his way out the door, "I love golf more than I love you. But," he proclaimed, "I love you more than tennis."

8. As Manny and Lou were unloading their gear at the golf club, a funeral procession passed by. Turning, Manny doffed his hat and paused as the cortege rolled past.

Surprised, Lou remarked, "That was a right sensitive thing for you to do, Manny. I never knew y'had it in you."

Manny shut the trunk of the car. "It was the least I could do. A week from tomorrow would have been our fortieth anniversary."

9. Zelda greeted her husband as he came home from a morning of golf. "How was your game?"

"I hit two great balls," he said.

"Then why so glum? That's better than last week when you didn't hit any."

"Not really," he replied. "I only hit 'em because I stepped on a rake."

10. Bart and Andrew were playing golf, and, teeing off, Bart sliced to the left and sent his ball flying into the rough. Going after it, he found the ball nestled in a field of buttercups. Taking out his nine-iron, Bart started thrashing away at the buttercups, looking for his ball.

Suddenly Bart heard a woman's voice behind him. "What are you doing?"

Turning, he saw a lovely young woman dressed in a flowing white gown and a wreath of red roses around her head.

Bart said, "What's it any of your business?"

The woman replied, "I'm Mother Nature, and henceforth, for what you've done to my buttercups, you will become deathly sick for a full day whenever you eat butter."

With that the woman faded into a sunbeam and vanished. Astonished, Bart stumbled from the rough to find his partner and tell him what happened. Calling for Andrew, he heard his friend reply, "I'm over here, looking for my ball."

"Where? I can't see you!"

"In the pussywillows."

Bart screamed at the top of his lungs, "Christ, whatever you do don't swing your club!"

1. The schoolbell rang, and while the other students filed from Mr. Scott's English class, the new black student walked over to the teacher.

   "Mr. Scott," said the pupil, "c'you tell me where the library's at?"

   The pedagogue's features twisted with disgust. "Young man," he said sternly, "in this class we do *not* end our sentences in a preposition!"

   Shrugging, the youth said, "C'you tell me where the library's at, asshole?"

2. "Deirdre," said the second-grade teacher, "would you please use *I* in a sentence?"

   The little girl thought for a moment, then said, "I is—"

   "No," the teacher interrupted, "you always say, 'I *am*.' "

   Nodding, Deirdre went on, "I *am* the letter that comes after *H*."

3. "Teacher," said Edgar, "if I give a horse a drink, is it right to say I watered the horse?" The teacher said it was, and Edgar beamed, "In that case, I just milked the cat."

4. Leroy was having problems in English class, so his teacher decided to stop by on her way home to speak with his parents. When she rang the bell, Leroy answered.

"I'd like to talk to your mother or father," she said.

"Sorry, but they ain't here."

"Leroy!" she said, "what is it with your grammar?"

"Beats me," he replied, "but dad sure was pissed that they had t'go bail her out agin."

GYNECOLOGISTS   *See* DOCTORS and BIRTH CONTROL 6

1. The young woman settled down on the examining table, and her gynecologist said, "Tell me again, Ms. Pennyworth, exactly what happened?"

"Well," she said, blushing, "my boyfriend had his face . . . down there, and he got so wild his glasses fell in."

"His glasses?" said the doctor. "Well, let's just have a look." As he was peering inside, the gynecologist said, "You know, Ms. Pennyworth, I can't see a thing in here."

"That's odd," she said. "I can see you just fine."

2. Then there was the gynecologist who started going to an analyst because he was always feeling low.

3. The moron went to her gynecologist and said, "Dr. Goodstone, my husband and I have been trying for months to have a baby; I just don't know what's wrong."

With a reassuring smile the doctor said, "Let's see what we can do about that. If you'll just get undressed and lie down on the table—"

"All right," the moron answered, "though I'd prefer to have my husband's baby."

4. Then there was the gynecologist who gave up his practice to become a comedian. He decided it was simply time to see men crack up.

5. Q: What's the difference between a genealogist and a gynecologist?

A: A genealogist looks up your tree, but a gynecologist just glances into your bush.

6. Then there was the lovesick gynecologist who looked up an old girlfriend. . . .

7. Mrs. Dempsy had just moved to town, and one of the first orders of business was to see her new gynecologist. Lying down on the table, she waited patiently for the doctor to arrive.

When he walked in, he said only a few words of greeting before setting to work; appreciating a warm bedside manner, Mrs. Dempsy was predisposed against him from the start. However, things got worse when he said from under the sheet, "My, what a cavernously large vagina you have! My, what a cavernously large vagina you have!"

Livid, Mrs. Dempsy said, "'Please, doctor, you didn't need to say it twice!"

"I didn't say it twice. I didn't say it twice."

8. The middle-aged woman seemed sheepish as she visited Dr. Zamor.

"Come now," coaxed the gynecologist, "you've been seeing me for years! There's nothing you can't tell me."

"This one's kind of strange—"

"Let me be the judge of that," the doctor assuaged her.

"Well," she said, "yesterday I went to the bathroom in the morning and I heard a plink-plink in the toilet; when I looked down, the water was full of pennies."

"I see."

"That afternoon I went again and there were nickels in the bowl."

"Uh-huh."

"That night," she went on, "there were dimes and this morning, doctor, there were quarters! You've got to tell me what's wrong," she implored, "I'm scared out of my wits!"

The gynecologist put a comforting hand on her shoulder. "There, there, it's nothing to be scared about. You're simply going through your change."

HALLOWEEN

1. Little Joey dressed as a pirate for Halloween and went out trick-or-treating. When he rang Mrs. Bonelli's doorbell, the woman handed him a lollipop and looked around with mock terror. "And tell me, Captain Joey, where are your buccaneers?"

   "Under my buckin' hat," the boy replied.

THE HANDICAPPED

1. Mr. Rawson was sitting at the bar when the fellow perched on the stool next to his slid off. Feeling that there was no way the man would make it home on his own, Mr. Rawson managed to get the man's address from him, and, since the house was only a few blocks away, he decided they could walk it. Slipping an arm around his waist, they started toward the door. No sooner had they taken a few steps then the men's legs crumpled and he dropped. Mr. Rawson patiently helped him up and he dropped again; once outside he fell again and then a fourth time.

   The man mumbled something, but Mr. Rawson was in no mood to listen.

"Ya drunken bum," he complained. "Why the hell didn't you cut it out before you got so falling down drunk?"

When the man took two more steps and fell both times, the Good Samaritan decided that enough was enough. He simply threw his shoulders beneath the man and carried him home.

Rapping indignantly, he strode in when a woman answered the door and then unceremoniously dumped the man on the couch.

"Here's your husband," Mr. Rawson complained. "And if I were you, I'd have a serious talk to him about his drinking."

"I will," the woman promised. "But tell me," she went on, (looking outside) "where's his wheelchair?"

HAREMS

1. The sheik was delighted to have ten wives, although wife number ten got bored because she had it so soft.

2. Then there was the sultan who came to the tent early one night, causing his delightful brides to let out a frightened sheik.

HEAVEN

See THE BIBLE, CLERGY, HELL, RELIGION and BOXING 4, INFIDELITY 13, MASTURBATION 2, MOTION PICTURES 8, PREJUDICE 1

1. An attractive young lady with raven-black hair and wide eyes approached the gates of Heaven. Looking her over, St. Peter said, "And may I ask, young lady, if you are a virgin?"

"I am," was her demure reply.

Not wanting to appear distrustful but having to be cautious, St. Peter called over an angel to examine her. Several minutes later the angel returned.

"She's a virgin," the angel stated, "though I'm obliged to inform you that she *does* have seven small dents in her maidenhead."

Thanking him, St. Peter took his place behind the ledger and faced the girl. "Well, miss, we're going to admit you. What is your name?"

She replied sweetly, "Snow White."

2. As soon as Mrs. Jones arrived in Heaven she sought her husband, who had died several years before.

"Excuse me," she said, approaching St. Peter, "but I'm looking for my husband. I wonder if you can help me."

"What was his name?" St. Peter enquired.

"Harry . . . Harry Jones."

St. Peter stroked his chin. "There are many here who have that name. What else can you tell me about him?"

Blurting out the first thing that came to mind, she said, "Well, the last thing he said before he died was that if I were ever unfaithful to him, he would turn in his grave."

"Ah!" said St. Peter. "you're looking for Pinwheel Harry!"

3. In a dream Mr. Liss heard God talking to him, telling him to better his physical appearance as he had great plans for the man. Thus, the very next morning he went out and had a nose job, underwent a hair transplant, got contact lenses, went to a tanning salon, and bought a whole new outfit.

On the way home after his busy day, Mr. Liss heard an ominous rumbling in the heavens, and was struck by lightning; the next thing he knew he was in Heaven. Irked and surprised, he sought out God.

"Lord," he said, "I don't understand it! Why did you put me through all this trouble only to smite me?"

God shrugged. "Sorry," he said, "I didn't recognize you."

4. Jesus was strolling through Heaven when he

saw an old man sitting on a cloud, staring disconsolately into the distance.

"Old man," said Jesus, "this is Heaven! Why are you so sad?"

The old man didn't bother to turn as he said, "I've been looking for my son and haven't been able to find him."

Jesus said, "Tell me about it."

"Well," said the old man, still gazing at the sunlit horizon, "on earth I was a carpenter, and one day my son went away. I never heard from him again, and I was hoping I'd find him here, in Heaven."

His heart pounding suddenly in his chest, Jesus bent over the old man and said, "Father?"

The old man turned and cried, "Pinocchio?"

5. God was annoyed. Too many people were being admitted to Heaven, and He established a new criterion: No one could enter unless they knew what one of their faith's principal holidays was all about.

As it happened, three Christians died and were the first ones to have to submit to the new ruling. They approached St. Peter one at a time, and he asked the first, "What is Easter all about?"

The woman shifted from foot to foot. "That's . . . uh . . . er . . . a holiday where we color eggs and . . . and . . ."

Shaking his head, St. Peter sent the woman to Hell, and the next aspiring angel walked up.

St. Peter asked him, "What is Easter all about?"

"Well . . . ummm . . . it's about this bunny who goes around. . . ."

Sighing, St. Peter sent the Christian to Hell and motioned for the next one to approach.

"What is Easter all about?"

The old man cleared his throat. "That's when Jesus was crucified and, rising from the dead, came from within the cave—"

"Praise the Lord!" St. Peter said. "A learned and worthy soul!"

"—and when he saw his shadow," the man went on, "it meant there would be six more weeks of winter."

HELL

See HEAVEN

1. Mr. Brent was being walked through Hell by one of the devils. As they entered the cave that was to be his new home, Brent was delighted to find it filled with champagne bottles and beautiful women.

"Say," he muttered, "this doesn't look like a bad way to spend eternity."

The devil snickered as he closed the iron gate bheind Brent. "Sorry to disappoint ya, fellah."

"What do you mean?" Brent licked his lips, "I can't thank you enough! This is fantastic!"

"What I mean," said the horned creature, "is

that the bottles all have holes in the bottom . . . and the women don't."

2. While being shown to his eternal damnation in Hell, Mr. Breslin happened to pass a cave in which Mr. Trupin was making love to Bo Derek.

Tapping a devil on the shoulder, Breslin complained, "Hey, it isn't fair! I've been condemned to spend eternity up to my neck in hot lava, but this guy's screwing Bo Derek!"

Prodding Mr. Breslin on with his pitchfork, the devil roared, "And who are *you* to criticize Bo Derek's punishment?"

HILLBILLIES　　　　*See* MORONS and ADOPTION 1,
FISHING 1, GENIES 4,
THE MILITARY 6, VENTRILOQUISTS 2

1. One day the hillbilly decided to have his property cleared of trees. Calling in a woodsman, he explained that he wanted all the trees cut down, save for one proud oak.

"Forgive me for asking," said the woodsman, "but why do you want that one tree spared?"

The hillbilly grinned. " 'Cuz that's whar I had my first taste o' lovemakin'."

The woodsman smiled with understanding.

"Yup," the hillbilly continued, "and the whole time her mom was standin' just a few paces off."

The woodsman's eyes grew wide. "You're kidding! But—didn't her mother *say* anything?"

"Sure did," the hillbilly declared. "She said, "Baaaaaaa. . . .""

2. Because his son wasn't the brightest kid in the world, Old Joe took him to the outhouse one day to teach him how to urinate properly.

"Now you lissen good, Dan'l, 'cuz here's whatcha gotta do. One: Take out yer peniepipe. Two: Pull back the foreskin. Three: Pee. Four: Push back yer foreskin. Five: Put yer equipment back."

The boy said he understood, but the next day while he was working at his still, the man's wife came running over.

"Oh, Joe, Joe, come quickly! Dan'l went t'piss an' he won't come outta the outhouse!"

"Hell, what's he doin' in there?"

"I dunno. He just keeps sayin' 'Two-four, two-four. . . .""

3. The hillbilly said to his city friend, "Guess what, Rufus? I found a condom on the patio."

The city boy asked, "What's a patio?"

4. The young hillbilly had just gotten married and, nervous about his wedding night, snuck out and paid his father a visit.

"Pop," he drawled, "Ah'm jest no sure Ah know what t'do."

"It's simple," said his father. "Remember the stiff thing y'used t'play with as a boy? Just take it out and stick it where yer honey pisses."

Filled with confidence, the boy ran home and, grabbing his baseball bat, threw it into the outhouse.

5. "So tell me," the city slicker asked the hillbilly, "is Boone's Hollow a healthy place to live?"

"You betcha!" crowed the lanky man. "Why, when I first got here I couldn't walk or take solid food."

"No kidding!" replied the visitor. "What was wrong?"

"Nuthin'," shrugged the hillbilly. "I was born here."

6. Q: Why shouldn't you take shit from a hill billy?
A: It might be his lunch.

7. Then there was the shotgun wedding, which for the young hillbilly in question was a case of wife or death.

8. Junius and Snuffy were sitting by the stream, fishing and trying to top each other. After exhausting tales about whose father could shoot the best or whose brother had loved more women, Junius said, "Y'know, the men in *my*

family are so tough that they eat their meat raw. Bet your'n don't."

"Yer right," Snuffy agreed. "They only *swaller* it raw. Then they sit in a fire to barbecue it."

HOCKEY   *See* BASEBALL, BOXING,
FOOTBALL, GOLF, SOCCER, WRESTLING

1. Hortense was watching the local news and turned to her husband, who was involved in a crossword puzzle. "Darling," she said, "did you hear that? A man in New York swapped his wife for a season pass to the Islanders' games. Would you do a thing like that?"

   "Hell, no," he replied. "The season's half over."

2. Then there was the hockey team that drowned during spring training. . . .

HOMOSEXUALS

See BISEXUALS, TRANSVESTITES and THE BIBLE 2, BOY SCOUTS 1, CHESS 3, CLERGY 17, DOGS 2, DWARFS 3, ESKIMOS 2, THE FBI 1, FLOWERS 2, FOOTBALL 2, INDIANS 6, SEX 2

1. A gay masochist is a sucker for punishment.

2. Then there was the gay boy who left home because he didn't like the way he was being reared.

3. And of course, it's common knowledge that most gays have mustaches in order to hide the stretch marks.

4. While patrolling a barren stretch of highway, a state trooper was surprised to find a naked young man tied to a tree. Pulling over, the trooper asked the youth to tell him what happened.

   "Well," he said, "I picked up this hitchhiker, and as soon as he got in he pulled a gun on me and took my car, wallet, and clothes. Then he did *this* to me."

   Unzipping his fly, the trooper chuckled, "Son, this just isn't your day."

5. Because of a bad case of hemorrhoids, the gay man went to his doctor. The physician prescribed

suppositories, but when it came time to use them the young man was afraid he'd botch the job. So he went into the bathroom and, bending over, looked through his legs at the mirror to line up his target.

All of a sudden, his penis became stiff and blocked his view.

"Oh, stop it," the young man chastised his organ, "it's only *me!*"

6. "It's not so bad," Mrs. Griswold said to her neighbor. "My Jack may be gay, but at least he's going with a doctor."

7. Two coeds agreed to room together, neither knowing that the other was a lesbian. Unfortunately, due to a mixup, there was only one bed in the room, and they were forced to share it.

Lying there, her heart thumping in her chest, one of the girls snuggled close to the other and said, "Listen, I'll be frank—"

"No," whispered the other girl, "let me be Frank. You can be Tom."

8. Q: How do you make a fruit cordial?
A: Pat him on the behind.

9. "And how do you know," said the principal, "that Tommy Edwards is gay?"

"He tried to butter me up."

10. Then there was the famous Scottish gay activist, Phil McCrevis . . .

11. . . . who, as fate would have it, took a job at the sperm bank. Sadly, he was fired a few days later for drinking on the job.

12. Having picked George up in a gay bar, Sandy was driving home when, entranced by his companion, he failed to see the red light. Piling into a van, he nearly marked his laundry when the driver got out, a big brute of a man.

   "You son of a bitchin' idiot!" he screamed. "You drive like my grandmother, and you can kiss my ass!"

   Sighing with relief, the gay driver said to his companion, "Thank God! He wants to settle out of court."

13. Ex-lovers Maurice and Timothy happened to bump into each other at a gay bar.

   "So," said Timothy, "how's your ass?"

   "Just *shut up!*" Maurice shot back.

   Timothy nodded. "Mine too. Must be some kind of allergy."

14. Father Reynolds wasn't the brightest guy in the world, and when he went in for an operation on his rectum the doctors decided to kill two birds with one stone. That morning an unwed mother had left her baby boy on the doorstep;

the doctors simply told Reynolds that by some miracle he had been pregnant and the infant was his.

Years passed, and the lad grew to manhood. Finally Father Reynolds lay on his deathbed.

"My boy," he said, "I have a confession to make. I . . . I am not really your father. I am your mother."

"My mother?" he exclaimed. "Then who is my father?"

"Monsignor Adams," he replied.

15. Though he was skillful using a salami in their lovemaking, nothing was so exciting to Joe's lover as when he cooed, "Hang on, darling . . . the wurst is yet to come!"

HONEYMOONS

See MARRIAGE, SEX

1. The newlyweds walked up to the hotel clerk and asked for a suite.

"Bridal?" asked the clerk.

The new bride flushed and said, "No, thanks. I'll hold his shoulders till I get the hang of it."

2. Then there was the new bride who was so exhausted on her wedding night that she just couldn't stay awake for a second.

3. On her wedding night the anxious bride said to her husband, "Charles, I hope you'll be gentle. I want you to know this is my first time."

"Your first time!" he exclaimed. "But you've been married three times before!"

"I know," she replied, "but my first husband was a drunk and could never perform, my second husband turned out to be gay, and my third husband was in advertising."

"The first two I understand," stated Charles, "but why didn't your third husband ever sleep with you?"

The wife replied, "All he ever did was sit on the bed and tell me how great it was going to be."

4. The new bride turned to her husband as they entered the bridal suite of the hotel.

"Honey," she said, "I must confess that I haven't any idea what to do tonight."

"Dear," her husband snickered, "you're putting me on."

5. It was a May-December marriage, and as the old man climbed into bed for the first time with his new bride, he asked, "Did your mother tell you what to do on your wedding night?"

"Yes," she said, kissing him on the forehead, "everything."

"Good," said the elderly gentleman as he turned out the light, "because I've forgotten."

6. As they entered the honeymoon suite, the woman said to her new husband, "Dear, which side of the bed would you like to sleep on?"

Scratching his head, the dull-witted sot replied, "The top side, I guess."

7. "Tell me," the husband asked his wife on their wedding night, "am I the first man you ever slept with?"

"No," the woman shook her head, "I'd have recognized you when we met."

8. As it happened, their wedding night fell during a religious holiday, and, devout Episcopalian that he was, Mr. Rogers simply couldn't make love to his virginal bride.

"I'm sorry," he said as they snuggled in bed, "but I can't have you tonight. It's Lent."

Her brow crinkling with concern, Mrs. Rogers said, "Okay . . . but to whom and for how long?"

9. Trying to think of an unusual wedding gift to get for their daughter and son-in-law, the Hemingways decided to buy a tape recorder, slip it under their bed, and present them with a permanent record of their first night together.

Bribing a bellhop at the hotel, they got the tape recorder in and out and—curiousity getting the best of them—they decided to listen to the tape before turning it over.

"That's happiness," they heard their daughter moan when they switched it on. *"That's* happiness!"

"Wait a minute," said Mr. Hemingway, "that red light means the batteries are low."

Fixing the machine, they rewound it and listened again at the correct speed; only this time they heard their daughter chuckling, "That's a penis? *That's* a penis?"

10. Then there were the newlyweds who left the reception early so they could put their things together. . . .

11. Poking her head from the bathroom of their honeymoon suite, the young bride asked, "Would you like me to wear my new black teddy?"

Sighing, her impatient husband replied, "I would like nothing better."

12. Lying in bed on their wedding night, the husband called to his rather naive wife, who was standing on the balcony of the hotel.

"My dear," he said softly, "aren't you coming to bed?"

"No," she replied. "I've always heard that this will be the most beautiful night of my life, and I don't want to miss a moment of it!"

13. Returning to the office after her honeymoon, Stella confided in her best friend, "There we

were, making love for the first time, when someone knocked on the door of the hotel room. And
can you believe it? Jack got up to answer it."

"You mean he got out of bed and left you
lying there?"

"That's just it," Stella complained, "he took
me with him!"

14. Upon returning from their honeymoon, Mrs.
Gilliam turned to her husband and asked, "Would
you like me to put on the kettle for you?"

Grining, Mr. Gilliam said, "I'd prefer that
black teddy you wore on our wedding night."

HORSES   *See* ANIMALS

1. Mr. Thomas owned the fleetest young stallion
in the state, but there was a problem: Every
time he raced, the colt would slow down in
order to wink at the mares. Deciding that there
was only one way to protect his investment in
the animal, Mr. Thomas had the horse gelded.

The surgery was performed, and a few weeks
later the horse was back in the gate. Sure enough,
his eye didn't wander: His head bent low, eyes
intense, the animal had only the track in mind.

The gun sounded and the horse bolted from
the gate, but after a few paces it stopped, turned,
and ran back.

Mr. Thomas bolted from the stands. "Jesus, what's wrong?" he shouted as he neared the horse.

"What's wrong?" the horse said testily. "How would you feel if you stepped from the gate and some wise guy yelled into the loudspeaker, 'They're off!'?"

2. Q: What's the difference between maids and off-track betting?
A: Maids are people who clean windows.

3. Josiah owned the most unflappable horse in the Midwest and, deciding to make some money off him, brought the stallion to the county fair. There he offered five hundred dollars to anyone who could make the animal laugh.

Person after person came up to the horse, paying Josiah five dollars for every minute they spent with the animal. Most stood in front of the animal and made funny faces, some did tricks, a few even told jokes, but the horse didn't crack a smile. By the end of the day Josiah had made five hundred dollars and was looking forward to reaping a small fortune.

Just before closing time, a dwarfish little man came up. He handed Josiah a five-dollar bill, climbed on a stool, cupped his hand to the animal's ear, and whispered something; at once, the animal broke into a fit of mirthful neighing and whinnying. Shocked, Josiah handed over the five hundred dollars he had made and resolved to change his tactics.

The next day Josiah decided to offer five hundred dollars to anyone who could make his horse cry. Person after person tried and by day's end, Josiah had recouped the money he had lost. Just then the same dwarfish man showed up. Taking his money, Josiah watched as the little fellow stood in front of the horse and dropped his pants. At once the horse began to weep uncontrollably.

Hitching up his pants, the short man collected his money and started away. Bursting with curiosity, Josiah called after him.

"Wait a minute, ya puny thing, I gotta know. What made my horse act like that?"

"Simple," said the dwarfish man. "Yesterday, I told him my penis was bigger than this. Today," he shrugged, "I showed him."

HOSPITALS

1. Mr. Harrison was feeling run-down and his doctor decided to put him into the hospital for some tests.

   After the first few tests had been completed, a nurse came in and offered Mr. Harrison some soup. But he was tired and refused it, subsequently falling asleep.

Shortly thereafter the results of the first tests came back, and the doctor determined that his patient's problem was simply severe constipation. Waking him up and ordering an enema on the groggy patient, the doctor watched with satifaction as Mr. Harrison's health swiftly improved; the following morning Mr. Harrison was released.

"How was your stay?" his wife asked as she picked him up.

"Fine," he replied, "but if you ever have to stay here, make sure you eat the soup."

"The soup?" she said. "Is that what cured you?"

"No," he answered, "but if you *don't* eat it, they make you take it up the ass."

2. Dr. Roche was such a busy man that at the hospital he only had time to scribble abbreviations on the patients' charts. *T* stood for tonsillectomy, *OH* was open heart surgery, *BS* meant brain surgery, and so on.

As was his habit, Dr. Roche also greeted new interns as soon as they arrived. Unfortunately, he was a little late in getting to Dr. Cohen. Greeting the intern in the corridor after surgery, he asked, "So, Dr. Cohen, how did Mrs. Gaines's appendectomy go?"

Cohen paled. "Appendectomy? I thought you wanted an autopsy."

3. Then there's the home surgery kit called Suture Self. . . .

4. Dr. Churchill was walking down the hospital corridor when suddenly his patient Mr. Barnes came running by, his hands cupping his genitals. Hot on his heels was Nurse Torquemada carrying a still-steaming tea kettle.

   Catching the nurse by the arm, the doctor yelled, "Hold it, nurse, you misunderstood! I said *prick* his *boil*"!"

5. Mr. Stevens rushed his daughter Maybelle to the hospital after she swallowed a box of firecrackers. Shortly thereafter, Mrs. Stevens arrived.

   "How is she?" the woman asked.

   Her husband replied, "We've gotten favorable reports."

6. Walt had broken so many bones that it was necessary for him to wear a bodycast. During that time he had to be fed rectally.

   On his birthday the nurse decided to give him a treat by giving him some coffee through the food tube. Within instants Walt was screaming for her.

   "What's the matter!" she cried, "is it too hot?"

   "No," he shouted back, "I don't take it with sugar!"

7. Mr. Maggin put in an emergency call to the

hospital. "This is Elliot Maggin, and we're going to need a room. My wife's water just broke!"

"I see," said the nurse. "And is this her first child?"

"Hell, no," he said, "it's her husband!"

HOTELS   See CLERGY

1. The clerk of the fleabag hotel said, "Wouldja like a room with running water?"

   With a nasty frown the drunk replied, "What do I look like, a trout?"

HUNCHBACKS   See TAILORS 3

1. Upon the death of Quasimodo, the cathedral of Notre Dame advertised for a new bellringer. Much to the rector's surprise, the first person to answer the ad was a hunchback. However, he was different from the beloved Quasimodo in that he had no arms.

   After looking the fellow up and down, the perplexed clergyman asked, "My son, are you sure you can do the job?"

   In response the ambitious hunchback bolted past the rector and ran up the stairs. Reaching the bell tower, he positioned himself several paces from the colossal bell and hurled himself at it, striking the iron shell with his face. The cathedral filled with its glorious sound from crocket to lintel and, scampering back, the bruised but proud hunchback struck the bell again, once more using his face. Again the bell rang out and though his face was by this time bloodied and he was obviously dazed, the giddy hunchback ran at it yet again. This time, however, the disoriented fellow missed the bell entirely and plunged to his death.

Running from the cathedral, the priest fought through a gathering crowd in order to administer the last rites to the unfortunate hunchback. When he'd finished, a constable came over.

"Do you know who he is?" asked the officer.

"No," confessed the clergyman, "but his face rings a bell."

2. Notre Dame was still without a bellringer, and one afternoon the identical twin brother of the first hunchback came and applied for the job.

Staring at the armless fellow, the priest said, "My son, are you aware what happened to your poor brother?"

Nodding manfully, the hunchback dismissed the rector's fears with an arrogant toss of his head and took his place in the bell-tower. Charging the bell he too struck it with his face and produced a sound as strong and majestic as that of his brother. Stepping back, he ran at it again, his battered countenance filled causing the air to be with a full-bodied *gong*.

So as not to repeat his brother's fatal error, the hunchback mustered his concentration for the third strike, staring hard at the bell. However, the poor hunchback failed to see the ledge of the bell tower behind him and fell to his death in the street.

Hurrying to the dead hunchback's side, the rector repeated the sad ritual and rose to face the approaching constable.

"And did you know *this* one?" the officer asked.

"No," answered the clergyman, "but he's a dead ringer for his brother."

HUNTERS   See ANIMALS 9 and CANNIBALS 4

1. Q: Why do hunters make the best lovers?
   A: Because they go deep into the bush, shoot more than once, and always eat what they shoot.

2. Then there was the hunter who didn't want to shoot craps because he didn't know how to cook them.

3. Hurrying back to camp after a day on the veldt, one hunter said to another, "Jesus, there's a giraffe out there with three balls! What should I do?"

After reflecting for a moment, the other hunter replied, "Walk him and pitch to the hippo."

4. Upon learning that the available young man was a devotee of hunting, Andrea did what any girl in her position would have done: She told him she was game. . . .

5. The moron and his best friend Tony were out hunting ducks when suddenly a magnificent mallard flew overhead. Shouldering his rifle, Tony blasted it from the sky.

"Great shot, huh?" he said.

"It sure was," said the moron, "but you wasted a bullet."

"What are you talking about?"

"The fall alone would've killed it."

6. Tired of hearing how he was the greatest shot in the state, Frank bet Oscar that if they went in the woods, he could find an animal he couldn't hit. Oscar's ego was such that he accepted the bet willingly, and the next morning the two men went tramping through the woods.

Suddenly Frank spotted a squirrel at the top of a distant tree. The towering oak had to be a thousand yards away . . . beyond the range of his companion's shotgun. "There," he said. "Hit that squirrel."

Taking aim, Oscar fired; an instant later the squirrel scurried down the tree.

Frank beamed. "Well, ole pal, looks like you lose."

"Lose?" Oscar declared. "You just witnessed a miracle."

"What miracle is that?"

"A squirrel runnin' with its heart shot out."

7. Still perspiring with fear, the hunter told the friend back at camp, "Here I was with this thirteen-foot grizzly hot on my tail, snorting hard and out for blood. My gun was out of ammo, and the only refuge in sight was a tree whose lowest branch was twenty feet off the ground."

"Do you mean to say that you actually managed to jump up and grab that branch?"

"On my way down," the shaken hunter replied.

HYPNOTISM

1. While delivering a fiery sermon one Sunday morning, Father Lowell happened to notice a glazed look in the eyes of each and every parishioner. Realizing that this wasn't their typical bored stupor, he deduced that the congregation had actually been hypnotized by the swaying of the new gem-encrusted crucifix he wore about his neck.

Performing a little experiment, he told the

transfixed worshipers to put all of their money in the collection plate—and, lo and behold, that's exactly what they did. Delighted, Father Lowell gave an equally impassioned sermon the following week, and once again the swaying cross mesmerized the crowd, and, at his suggestion, they turned over all their money.

Going for the triple crown, Father Lowell gave another inspired sermon the following week. However, he became so caught up that he momentarily forgot himself and, gesturing broadly, overturned a goblet of wine. Looking down at the mess, he snapped, "Shit!"

That afternoon the church had to be condemned.

IMMIGRANTS   *See* ACCENTS and UNEMPLOYMENT 4, 5

1. Severely constipated, the immigrant went to the doctor and was given a prescription for suppositories. Never having used them in the old country, the immigrant proceeded to eat one a day for a week.

Still constipated, he went back to the doctor who looked at him with amazement.

"I can't believe it, Janos. A week of these and you *still* haven't moved your bowels." He threw up his hands. "Are you sure you used the entire box?"

Snarling with disgust, Janos said, "Whadda hell you *think* I do, shova dem up my ass?"

2. Then there was the Hungarian immigrant who upon entering the U.S. was asked, "Ms. Olt, have you had a checkup recently?"

"No, dalink," she replied, "but I've had a few Romanians."

3. Unable to move his bowels, the immigrant went to visit the doctor. Writing out a prescription for a powerful laxative, the doctor instructed the immigrant to return for a checkup two days hence.

When the immigrant returned, the doctor asked, "Well, have you moved yet?"

Stating that he had not, the immigrant was advised to double the dosage and return in two days. On the appointed day the immigrant showed up and once again advised the doctor that he hadn't moved; and once again the doctor doubled the dosage. Finally, on his fourth visit, the immigrant entered smiling.

"I take it you've moved?" enquired the doctor.

The immigrant nodded vigorously. "I had to," he said. "My apartment was full of shit."

1. When the Indian Chief found his daughter sleeping with one of the tribe's braves, he was furious.

   "Because you slept with my daughter," he roared, "you must marry her. But first, you must pass a test of courage to show that you're worthy."

   "Anything," said the bold young buck.

   At the chief's instructions, the brave hacked a hole in the ice of a frozen lake. "Now," said the chief, "you must swim the mile across and back. If you succeed, you may marry my daughter."

   Without hesitation, the young Indian jumped in; by nightfall he hadn't returned and was presumed dead.

   The young squaw was distraught, and to atone for his vengeful act the chief named the lake after the brave, a name it retains to this day: Lake Schmuck.

2. Then there was the equally shortsighted brave who, after having his manhood bound in leather for a rite of passage, queried the chief, "How come?"

3. It's a little-known fact, but years before Thomas Edison invented the light bulb, an Indian brave named Wise Buck performed a similar scientific

miracle. Whenever they'd use the outhouse at night, the Indians would stumble about and make a racket, waking everyone else at the settlement. Thus, using principles set down by Benjamin Franklin, the clever Indian strung the john with electric lights. In fact, Wise Buck was the first person in history who ever wired a head for a reservation.

4. A young Indian boy approached his father. "My father," he asked, "I would like to know how all of us got our names."

Smiling benevolently, the Indian brave said, "Son, it's very simple. Your grandfather was born when the sun was just coming up, so he was called Rising Sun. I was born during a great storm, so he named me Black Cloud. But tell me," the Indian paused, "why do you ask all of this, Hole-in-Rubber?"

5. An Iroquois Indian named Brown Elk walked into the saloon. He was a giant of a man with a six-shooter tucked in his belt, so no one dared ask why he was carrying a pail of manure in one hand and a small cat in the other.

"I'll have a whiskey," he told the bartender, and after downing the shot Brown Elk ordered another. Then another. Finally, after his fourth drink, the Iroquis pulled out his revolver, fired several shots into the bucket, released the cat, then ran after it. When he caught it, he returned to the bar.

"E-Excuse me," said the alarmed bartender, serving him a drink on the house, "but would you mind telling me what that w-was all about?"

"My father told me to try and be more like white man," he answered. "So I came here to have a few drinks, shoot the shit, and chase a little pussy."

6. Then there was the gay Indian named Brave Sucker. . . .

7. His lover was the famous three-testicled Indian, Buck-and-a-Half.

8. Then there was the Indian who preferred tea to firewater. Unfortunately, he drank too much one night and drowned in his tea pee.

INFIDELITY
See BIGAMY, MARRIAGE, SEX
and DISEASE 9, FITNESS 1,
HEAVEN 2, MURDER 1, SLEEP 1, SUICIDE 2

1. Then there was the exceedingly jealous husband who had a vasectomy but didn't tell his wife until she was pregnant.

2. "Do you want the bad news first or the terrible news?" the lawyer asked Mr. Tamarind.

"Hell, give me the bad news first."

"The bad news it that your wife found a picture worth a hundred thousand dollars."

"That's *bad* news?" asked Mr. Tamarind. "In that case, I can't wait to hear the terrible news."

"The terrible news is that it's of you and your secretary."

3. "Well," the woman asked the detective she'd hired, "did you trail my husband?"

"Yes I did, ma'am. I followed him to a bar, a disco, and then to an apartment."

A big smile crossed the woman's face. "Then I've got him! Is there any question about what he was doing?"

"No ma'am," said the detective. "I'm sure he was following you."

4. Two longtime business acquaintances were walking down the street when suddenly one of the men turned to the other, looking very distressed.

"My God!" he said, averting his face, "here come my wife and my mistress *together*!"

"Christ," said the other, also turning away, "mine too."

5. Then there was Mr. Ogan, who went into a store to buy a fur coat. "It's for my wife," he told the clerk. However, Mrs. Ogan happened to see him . . . so it was.

6. He was almost as hapless as the coal miner whose wife divorced him because he came home with a clean dick.

7. Q: If a spouse is one mate, what are two or more mates?
    A: Spice.

8. Upon returning home from the office party at the crack of dawn, Jake was greeted by his angry wife.

   "Darling!" he exclaimed, "why did you leave so early?"

   "Your behavior was disgusting," she snapped, "and before I call a lawyer, I want to know just one thing: Who was that woman I saw you outwit last night?"

9. After spending the day with her father at his office, little Carla asked over dinner, "Daddy, when your office door was closed, I was looking through the keyhole. Why did you call your secretary a doll?"

   Under his wife's stormy gaze the man said quickly. "Uh, well, Carla, it's just an expression. It's because I enjoy having her around. She works the word processor like a pro, is disarming when she answers the telephone, is never late, and always eats her lunch at her desk."

   "Oh," said the girl. "I thought it was because

she closed her eyes when she lay down with you on the couch."

10. After having been unfaithful for years, Jim told his business partner Vinnie that he was going to come clean with his wife and beg for her forgiveness. The only thing Vinnie cautioned was that he not reveal the names of his paramours, since it wasn't fair to get them in trouble.

    Confessing his infidelity that night, Jim was surprised when his wife's curiosity outweighed her anger.

    "Tell me," she demanded, "who did you sleep with? Was it that hussy Mrs. Kelleher?"

    "I can't tell you," Jim replied.

    "I know. It was that slut Loree. She's slept with everyone in town!"

    "Discretion forbids," he begged off.

    "Mrs. Kieffer," she said confidently. "You went to bed with that whore!"

    Once again Jim said nothing and his wife gave up. The next day Vinnie asked him how things went.

    "Terrific," Jim replied. "Not only did my wife forgive me, but she gave me three new leads!"

11. Then there was the married radio buff who was more concerned with frequency than with fidelity.

12. While Ronald was visiting his old buddy Jim

and his wife Paula, a terrible snowstorm hit town, stranding him at the apartment. Since there wasn't a spare bed or even a couch, the couple invited him to share their king-size bed.

Shortly after Jim fell asleep, Paula motioned for Ronald to come over. Paula was certainly a fetching creature, and Ronald wanted her—but he was afraid that Jim might wake up.

"Nothing wakes him," Paula tried to allay his fears. "If you don't believe me, pull a hair from his ass. He won't budge."

Though dubious, Ronald did what she suggested and, sure enough, Jim didn't stir. Encouraged, he slipped over to Paula's side of the bed and made love to her. A half hour later she wanted him again: once again pulling a hair from his friend's ass to make sure he was alseep, Ronald made love to her a second time.

They passed the night that way, Ronald yanking a hair from Jim's ass each time he prepared to make love to Paula. However, after the sixth time Jim finally opened his eyes.

"Y'know, friend," he complained, "I really don't mind you screwing my wife, but I sure as hell wish you'd stop using my ass as a scoreboard."

13. "Mother," said the little girl, "do people go to Heaven feet-first?"

"Why no," her mother replied, "whatever made you think that?"

"Well," she said, "last night while you were out, the maid kept screaming, 'God . . . oh, God, I'm coming!' And she was jumping around so much that if daddy hadn't been lying on top of her, I'll bet she would have."

14. Mr. Buba returned home early one day to find a stranger straddling his naked wife, his head between her ample bosom.

"Say," the irate husband demanded, "just what are you doing?"

"Why, uh, er . . . I'm listening to music."

"Music?" said Mr. Buba. Placing his head beside that of the stranger, he declared, "I don't hear any music!"

"Of course you don't," the resourceful fellow extemporized. "You aren't plugged in."

15. Clancey had been on a business trip and, finishing up a day early, sent his wife a telegram saying that he'd be home that evening. Upon his arrival the businessman was shocked to find his wife in bed with another man; storming out, he went straight to his lawyer's house to see about a divorce.

"I know you're upset," attorney Gingold said as he fixed him a drink, "but don't you think you're being a little hasty? Why don't you call and see if there's some kind of explanation?"

Not wanting to flush ten years of marriage down the drain, Clancey reluctantly called his wife. "Well?" he said. "Why did I find you in the arms of another man?"

His wife replied forthrightly, "Because the telegram just arrived."

16. Esther and Jonas were making passionate love when Esther heard a sound in the driveway.

"Omigod, that's my husband."

"Shit," Jonas moaned as he leapt from bed and pulled on his pants, "where's the back door?"

"We don't *have* a back door!" Esther shot back.

"I see. Where do you want it?"

17. Having gone to his secretary's apartment, Mr. Biggs was astonished to wake up and find that it was 3:00 A.M. "Christ," he exploded, "my wife will kill me!"

Quickly calling home, he was struck with sudden inspiration. When his wife answered, he panted into the phone, "Darling, don't pay the ransom. I've escaped!"

18. The woman broke from a tangled embrace to answer the phone. When she hung up, her companion asked who it was.

"My husband," she replied, kissing him on the nose. "He was calling to say he'd be out late because he went bowling with you."

19. Then there was the adulterous husband who was too good to be true. . . .

20. Lunching with her friend, Miriam said, "I've got to be extra careful not to become pregnant these days."

"I don't understand," said the friend. "I thought your husband went for a vasectomy."

"Exactly," winked Miriam.

INFLATION   *See* FINANCE, BUSINESS
                                 and GOLF 4

1. As he was leaving the supermarket, Mr. Danton noticed the sign that said "Return Empties Here." So he went back and dropped off his wallet.

2. Inflation has caused stores to adapt as well as consumers. Signs that used to read "Watch your Children" now read "Watch Your Language."

3. Mrs. Kelley finally decided that nowhere on earth was inflation more unjust than at the butcher shop. It was the only place she paid an arm and a leg and came away with a leg.

4. However, there was one advantage to Mrs. Kelley's day of grocery shopping. That night, she and her family had a religious experience: the Last Supper.

5. Then there was the pundit who explained the ups and downs of the economy as the result of having elected so many yo-yos.

INSECTS

See ANIMALS, WORMS and RESTAURANTS 6, SAMURAIS 1

1. Q: What's the last thing that goes through a bug's mind when it hits the windshield?
   A: Its ass.

2. Then there was the not very bright mosquito who bit the buxom lass on the neck. . . .

3. Encountering a grasshopper during a long walk through the country, Dr. Doolittle bent beside the little green fellow and said, "Did you know, my insect friend, that they've named a drink after you?"
   "No kidding!" he replied. "You mean they've named a drink Ed?"

4. Then there's the new "no frills" pesticide that doesn't kill flies but makes them horny. That way, people can swat two at once.

5. Rufus went to the store and bought a box of mothballs; the following day he returned for a dozen more boxes.

"Say," said the clerk, "didn't you just buy a box yesterday?"

"I did," said Rufus, "but damn, those moths fly so fast they're tough to hit!"

6. Then there was the fly who left the toilet seat because he got pissed off.

7. Q: How many fleas does it take to screw in a light bulb?

   A: Two. The trick is getting them inside. . . .

8. Then there was the termite who sauntered into the saloon and asked, "Is the bar tender here?"

JOGGING

1. Finding that his sexual stamina was on the wane, the middle-aged man went to his doctor to ask his advice.

   "Your wind is bad, and you're out of shape," the doctor replied. "I suggest jogging five miles a day."

   Though he hated all forms of exercise, the man reluctantly agreed. A week later he phoned his physician.

   "So? How do you feel?"

   "Great!" the man cheered.

   "And how's your sex life?"

"How should I know?" the patient replied, "I'm thirty-five miles from home."

2. After completing his run through the park, Wallace threw himself on the grass and did some pushups. Just then a moron happened by.

"I hate to say it," the moron offered, "but I think she slipped away."

JUDGES

See CRIME, JURIES, LAWYERS and DIVORCE 2, OFFICE 11

1. Q: What has eighteen legs and a pair of tits?
   A: The Supreme Court.

2. After listening to the elderly hooker plead her case, Judge Hand called a brief recess and retired to his chambers. En route, he bumped into Judge Foote.

"Say," said Hand, "what would you give a sixty-three-year-old hooker?"

"Christ," replied Foote, "five or six bucks tops."

3. Then there was the old man brought up on charges of sexually molesting a teenager. However, the judge dismissed the case because the evidence wouldn't stand up in court.

4. Worse was the alleged rapist who stood before the judge and pleaded innocence by reason of insanity.

   "Insanity?" coughed the judge. "Young man,
   you seem perfectly normal to me."

   "Oh, I am," he admitted, "it's sex I'm crazy
   about."

5. Everyone in the courtroom waited with great
   anticipation as the judge, ensconced in his chambers, considered the evidence in the widely pub-
   licized paternity suit. Emerging after long minutes
   of deliberation, the brooding magistrate entered
   the courtroom and took his seat behind the bench.
   Staring at the defendant, he suddenly reached
   into his robes, withdrew a cigar, and with a
   flourish handed it to the young man.

   "Congratulations," the judge declared, "you've
   just become a father."

6. Looking down at the defendant, the judge said,
   "Mr. Riley, I've decided to give you a sus-
   pended sentence."

   Tears pouring from his eyes, Riley cried, "Oh,
   thank you, Your Honor!"

   "Don't thank me," the judge replied. "I'm
   sentencing you to be hanged."

7. Later that day the same judge meted out jus-
   tice yet again.

"I'm going to give you a short sentence," he said to the convicted murderer.

Grinning, the killer said, "*Bless* you, Your Honor."

"Life!" was the judge's edict.

"Life?" screamed the murderer. "But that's not a short sentence."

"They don't make 'em shorter than one word," was the judge's reply.

8. "Tell me again," asked the judge, "why you parked there?"

The moron rose and aswered respectfully, "Because, Your Honor, it said 'Fine for Parking.' "

JURIES

See CRIME, JUDGES

1. Since he was a Texan being tried in New York, the young man felt he didn't have a prayer of beating the murder rap. Thus, shortly before the jury was to retire he bribed one of the jurors to find him guilty of manslaughter.

The jury was out for days, after which they returned a verdict of manslaughter. Cornering the juror, the Texan said, "Thanks a million. How ever did you manage it?"

"It wasn't easy," admitted the juror. "The others wanted to acquit you."

(from Gemma Somers)

KIDS

See PARENTS and BATHROOMS 1, BIRTHDAYS 2, BLACKMAIL 1, CARD GAMES 4, CHRISTMAS 4, CLERGY 7, CLOTHING 3, CRIME 4, DOCTORS 5, DRUGS 1, FAT 4, FOUL LANGUAGE 1, HALLOWEEN 1, HILLBILLIES 2, 3, MATH 3, PETS 1, POLITICS 6, PROSTITUTES 8

1. Little Jimmy was a naughty little boy who, as it happened, wanted a bicycle more than anything else in the world. When he asked his mother for one, she told him that he could only have a bike if he learned to behave himself, which he promptly promised to do.

Alas, after a week of trying to behave, the boy found it next to impossible. Trying to be helpful, his mother suggested, "Maybe if you write a little note to Jesus, you'll find it easier to be good."

Jimmy agreed to try and, rushing upstairs, flopped down on his bed, pencil in hand.

"Dear Jesus," he wrote, "if you let me have a bike, I promise to be good for the rest of my life."

Realizing he could never do that, Jimmy crumpled the paper and started anew.

"Dear Jesus, if you let me have a bike, I promise to be good for a month."

Realizing that even *that* was beyond him,

Jimmy decided not to start again. Instead he ran into his mother's room, went to her dresser, removed her statue of the Holy Mother, closed it in a shoebox, and hid the shoebox under his bed. Hopping onto the bed, he returned to his pad and pencil.

"Dear Jesus," he wrote, "if you ever want to see your mother again. . . ."

2. On his first day home from his extracurricular classes for the gifted, little Sammy said to his father, "Daddy, what's sex?"

The boy's father turned red and went into a long, detailed explanation of the birds and the bees. When he was finished, Sammy pulled a questionnaire from his back pocket.

That's very interesting," he said, "but how'm I going to fit it all in this little box next to 'sex'?"

3. Breathless, the little girl ran in from playing. "Mommy, can little girls have babies?"

"Why, no!" replied the surprised mom.

"Thanks," the girl said, and as she ran out the door she called to her friends, "It's okay, we can play that game again!"

4. When the Jones family moved into their new house, a visiting relative asked five-year-old Sammy how he liked the new place.

'It's terrific," he said. "I have my own room,

Mike has his own room, and Jamie has her own room. But poor mom is still in with dad."

5. "Are you *sure* this money was lost?" the mother asked her son when he showed her the ten-dollar bill he'd found.

"Of course I'm sure!" he shot back. "I even saw the man looking for it!"

6. Mr. Baillie saw his son's shiner and demanded, "Scott, who gave you that black eye?"

"No one," replied the spunky lad. "I had to fight for it."

7. "Dad," asked little Roy, "do you have any idea why storks lift one leg when they eat?"

"Sure," dad replied. "If they lifted two, they'd fall over."

8. When Creighton was five years old and still hadn't uttered a single word, his parents decided to take him to a doctor. To make sure the boy was in a good humor, his mother made him an ice cream sundae. But she was so anxious about the appointment that she served him shaving cream instead of whipped cream. Taking a bite, Creighton suddenly spit out the food and snarled, "Hey, this sundae is terrible!"

His parents looked at him with astonishment. "Son," his father said, "you can speak! Why didn't you ever talk before?"

Creighton replied, "Everything's been fine till now."

9. It was summertime, and, to keep his dullard of a son out of trouble, Mr. Petrich gave him five dollars and sent him on a wild goose chase. "Take this," he said, "and buy me as much what's what as you can."

Nodding obediently, the young man set off. Since he had no mortal foggy notion what he was looking for, he figured it might be a food and stopped at the grocery store.

"Excuse me," he said to a clerk, "but I'd like to buy what's what."

Sensing that the boy was a real rube, the clerk decided to have some fun with him. Pointing across the street to a house with a red light, he said, "Fellah, you'll find what you're looking for there."

Thanking him and hustling over, the boy rang the bell. Much to his surprise, a voluptuous woman opened the door. She was naked, and, as he had never seen a woman's privates before, he stammered, "G-Gee, what's th-that?"

"What's what?" she asked.

The boy snapped back to reality. "Great!" he said. "Give me five dollars' worth."

10. Mr. Keene trudged through the snow to the home of his neighbor, Mr. Dahl.

"Awright," he snarled when Dahl answered

the door, "I've had it with your son pissin' in my yard. I looked out the window before and his name was written in the freakin' snow!"

Dahl grinned. "Come now, Keene . . . is that really worth getting all riled up about?"

"You bet," he replied. "It's my daughter's handwriting!"

LANDLORDS

1. Once there was the landlord who sent up heat religiously. He did it only on the sabbath.

LAWYERS   *See* JUDGES and INFIDELITY 2

1. The pope and an attorney arrived at the Pearly Gates at just the same time, and St. Peter showed them to their quarters. First the pope was taken to his room, a small, spartan cubicle with a chair, a desk, and a Bible. Then the lawyer was shown to his room, a massive duplex with women, wine, and a huge waterbed.

"Excuse me," said the lawyer to St. Peter, "there must be some mistake. Shouldn't the pope have this room?"

St. Peter shook his head. "No. We have dozens of popes in heaven, but you're our first attorney."

2. Then there was the aspiring lawyer who failed the bar exam because he thought an antitrust suit was a chastity belt.

3. After a heated exchange during a trial, the judge asked both counselors to approach the bench.

"Your Honor," said lawyer Cox, "I objected because my distinguished colleague was badgering the witness. It's obvious he's never heard of the Bill of Rights."

"Rubbish!" snapped attorney Updike. "I happen to know them by heart."

Cox cocked a disbelieving brow. "Do you, now? Well, Updike, I have a hundred dollars that says you can't even tell me the first few words."

Bristling, Updike accepted the challenge and began, "I pledge allegiance to the flag. . . ."

"Damn," Cox interrupted, fishing the money from his pocket, "I didn't think you'd know it."

4. "Tell me," said the personnel director of a large corporation, "are you an *honest* attorney?"

"Honest?" the lawyer replied. "Let me tell you something. My father lent me ten thousand dollars for my education, and I paid him back in full after my very first case."

"I'm impressed," he said. "And what case was that?"

The attorney squirmed slightly. "He sued me for the money."

5. Then there was the shark who refused to eat a lawyer out of professional courtesy.

6. The attorney strode confidently over to the witness. "Come now, Mr. Pendergast. It was nearly midnight, yet you say you saw my client strangle Mr. Pedigrew from nearly seven blocks away! Just how far can you see at night?"

Mr. Pedigrew shrugged. "I dunno. How far away is the moon?"

7. Q: What's the difference between a proud rooster and a lawyer?

A: The rooster clucks defiance. . . .

8. Then there was the lawyer who was so smart he never bothered to graduate; he settled out of class.

LEPERS
See DISEASE and GIGOLOS 3

1. The first time he went to a whorehouse, the leper enjoyed himself so thoroughly that he left his girl a tip.

2. Then there was the prostitute who contracted leprosy and her business started falling off.

3. Q: What do you call a leper in a bathtub?
   A: Stew.

4. Q: What goes ha-ha, ha-ha, thump?
   A: A leper laughing her head off.

5. However, there *is* one advantage to being a leper. If they're ever cut off by another motorist, they have no trouble giving the driver the finger.

LIBRARIANS

See BOOKS

1. The well-dressed young man walked up to the librarian as she was about to leave for her lunch break.

   "Madam," he said to the prim, spinsterly woman, "my name is Stephan, and I have a proposition for you. I'll wager five thousand dollars to your five hundred dollars that by this time tomorrow your nipples will be gone."

   The librarian was shocked but intrigued; the notion was preposterous, and she could certainly use the money.

   "You're serious?" she asked in her nasal voice.

   The young man withdrew the cash and lay it

on the counter. "Perfectly. Well, how about it? Are we on?"

Staring at the stack of crisp bills she replied, "We are," and the two shook hands on it.

For the rest of the day and all that night, the librarian kept her distance from every sharp utensil, especially the paper cutter, and at night enjoyed the rare extravagance of taking a cab home, lest she be accosted by some mad breast slasher. She ate cold tuna for dinner so she wouldn't have to light the gas range, and stayed up all night lest something bizarre befall her while she slept. The following morning, she was a bundle of frayed nerves as she waited for the young man to arrive.

Promptly at 11:45 A.M. Stephan walked in the door, just as he had the day before, only this time he was accompanied by a sharp-looking businessman. The librarian paid the businessman no attention, staring with wide, wild eyes at Stephan. Resting his hands on the counter, he smiled broadly at the librarian.

"Well?" he asked.

With a triumphant expression, the librarian tore open her blouse, yanking down her bra, and exposed her breasts. The nipples were intact. The businessman passed out, at which point Stephan handed the librarian five-thousand dollars; bending, he removed a thick wad of bills from the businessman's pocket.

"What's wrong with him?" the librarian asked.

"Simple," Stephan smiled. "I bet *him* twenty thousand dollars I could walk in here and have you show me your tits."

MAGICIANS

1. Dummo the Great was a terrific magician, but he wasn't very bright. He gave up a promising career with the circus and moved into a brothel because he heard they got a hundred dollars a trick.

MARRIAGE

See BIGAMY, HONEYMOONS, INFIDELITY, SEX and BIRTHDAYS 4, CANNIBALS 1, CARD GAMES 5, CHAUVINISM 4, CHRISTMAS 3, COOKING 1, DOCTORS 6, DRINKING 9, FARMERS 1, FLOWERS 1, GOLF 7, 8, HILLBILLIES 7, HOCKEY 1, MASTURBATION 2, MILLIONAIRES 1, 2, 3, MORONS 7, ROYALTY 1, 3, UNEMPLOYMENT 1

1. "You weren't in *one store* today?" said the disbelieving husband to his prodigal wife. "Tell me, *which* one?"

2. Sick of his wife's frigidity, the husband bought a big tube of K-Y Jelly and told his wife that it

would make her a happy woman. So it did. When he was out, she put it on the bedroom doorknob.

3. "They caught me with my best friend's wife," the disenhearted husband admitted to the bartender. "Now I'm on my own."

4. "What!" the irate husband screamed at his wife, "you're sleeping with my best friend?"

"Yeah," she taunted. "I bet you didn't even know he had it in for you!"

5. When the young groom came to bed on his wedding night, he was surprised to find a large padlocked chest at the foot of the bed.

"What's that for?" he asked his wife.

She wouldn't tell him, saying only that the contents were a secret she could never share with him. Reluctantly her gallant husband honored her privacy and considered the odd matter closed.

Years passed, and finally, on their fiftieth wedding anniversary, the husband's curiosity got the best of him. He approached his wife and literally begged her to tell him what was inside the chest. Gazing into his pleading eyes, she smiled and agreed to open the chest.

Fetching the key, she raised the lid: Inside were two ears of corn and fifty thousand dollars.

"Corn?" said the surprised old man. "What in heaven's name is that for?"

"Well," his wife confessed, "every time I cheated on you I put an ear of corn in the chest."

The man looked from his wife to the chest. He was surprised to learn that she'd been unfaithful, but he had to admit that twice in fifty years wasn't too bad. He smiled.

"I understand," he said softly. "And the fifty thousand dollars? What's that for?"

She replied, "Every time I had a bushel, I sold it."

6. The attractive young woman lay back on the psychiatrist's couch. "Oh, Doctor," she said, "I can't believe it. I've just married for the third time, and I'm still a virgin."

"Still a virgin!" gasped the doctor as he stared at the beautiful woman. "My word, how can this be?"

"Well," the woman sighed, "my first husband was a professor, and he only talked about it. My second husband was a physician, and he only looked at it."

"And your third husband?" asked the doctor. "What's *his* problem?"

"He's a gourmet."

7. Upon coming home from work, Mr. Cramden

was surprised to find his wife sliding up and down the banister.

"And what," he asked, "are you doing?"

She shouted over her shoulder as she ran back up the stairs, "Just heating up your dinner."

8. Sitting in the sauna, starry-eyed Daniel sighed to a perfect stranger, "Y'know, my wife's an angel."

"I envy you," the other man snorted. "Mine's still alive."

9. On their twentieth wedding anniversary a couple took a trip to the old country. While driving through the Black Forest, they came upon a sign that said, "Wishing Well—next left."

Though dubious, the husband and wife took the next left and pulled over beside an old stone well. Getting out, the man read the instructions and, leaning over the well, threw in a penny and made a wish. Then his wife did likewise. However, when she leaned over she lost her balance, tumbled in, and drowned.

Stepping back, the man cheered, "Hey—it really works!"

10. Waking up after a restless night, the wife turned to her husband and frowned. "I can't believe it! All night long you kept cursing me in your sleep!"

The husband replied, "Who was sleeping?"

11. Then there was the man who walked a very straight line because his wife was the ruler.

12. There was another man who was so romantic he died for love: His wife caught him cheating and blew his brains out.

13. According to the sage, man is incomplete until he's married; then he's finished.

14. That same sage points out that most women like to pick and choose when it comes to marriage. They choose their husband, then spend the rest of their life picking on him.

15. "Oh, God," sighed the wife one morning, "I'm convinced my mind is almost completely gone!"

    Her husband looked up from the newspaper and commented, "I'm not surprised: You've been giving me a piece of it every day for twenty years."

16. Having dinner with his father on the day before his wedding, the young man said, "So, dad, any fatherly advice you can impart before the big day?"

    Chewing thoughtfully on his steak, the man replied, "There are just two things, son: First, tell her you've got to have one night a week to go out with the boys; and second, don't waste it on the boys."

17. Then there was the man who didn't know what true bliss was until he got married. Unfortunately, then it was too late.

18. "I just buried my second wife," the widower told his new secretary over lunch, "and I've vowed never to marry again."

"That's a shame," said the woman, "but you know—it helps to talk about these things. What happened to your wives?"

"Well," he sighed, "the first one died after eating poisoned mushrooms, and the second one was shot to death."

"Shot!" the secretary gasped, "how horrible."

"Yes," said her boss, "she wouldn't eat her mushrooms."

19. The middle-aged woman came back from her physical with a smile on her face.

"Why the grin?" asked her sour-faced husband.

"Because," she boasted, "Dr. Berkowitz told me I have the bust of a woman half my age."

"Oh, yeah? And what about your sixty-year-old ass?"

The woman answered, "Come to think of it, he didn't say a *thing* about you."

20. Quentin said to his wife over dinner, "Drinking makes you beautiful."

Puzzled, the woman said, "I don't drink."

"I know," said Quentin, "but I do."

MASSAGES

1. Perhaps the most unfortunate masseur of all was Marcel, who went out of business because he rubbed his customers the wrong way. . . .

MASTURBATION
See SEX and CARD GAMES 4, DRUGGISTS 6, ROYALTY 6

1. Q: What's the definition of masturbation?
   A: Sex with someone you love.

2. Mrs. Rooney died and went to Heaven, where, much to her surprise, she found the golden walls lined with clocks; under each was a person's name. As she was being shown around by an angel, she noticed a clock for Mr. Bevis the butcher, Mrs. Tolland the schoolteacher, Mr. Garf the police officer, and Mr. Carrington the mayor; but there was none for her husband.

   "Excuse me," she finally asked the angel, "but I must know: What are all of these clocks for?"

   "Oh," said the angel, blushing, "those tell us who on earth is masturbating. Each time someone fondles themselves, the clock skips ahead a full hour. That way, when they arrive, we know how many demerits they've earned."

Bursting with pride, she said, "I notice my Herbie doesn't need a clock."

"Actually," the angel replied, "that isn't quite true."

"Oh? Then where is it?"

Flushing again, the angel said, "It's in our office. We use it as a fan."

3. "I haven't been feeling myself today," Father Dietrich said to his colleague, Father Dunn.

"And a good thing too," Dunn replied. "It's an awful habit."

4. The minister entered the bathroom at the church, and while he was using the urinal he heard moaning coming from one of the stalls. Entering a stall beside the one whence the sounds were coming, he stood on the toilet seat and discreetly peeked over. There he saw Roger DeLeon masturbating.

Sneaking from the lavatory, the minister decided to have a chat with the boy. Waiting until he came out, he took Roger aside and without being harsh or judgmental said, "I happen to know what you were doing in there, Roger, and I must tell you that the boys whom God truly loves are those who save it until they're married."

Nearly a month passed before the minister happened to bump into Roger again. "And how are we doing with our . . . problem?" he asked.

"Great!" he answered. "So far I've saved nearly a quart."

5. Then there was the chronic masturbator who used both hands so he could enjoy group sex. . . .

6. And the man who found playing piano by ear less stimulating than fiddling with his dick.

MATH

1. Q: What's the square root of sixty nine?
   A: Ate something.

2. The teacher said to her class, "Maria got the highest grade on the Spanish test . . . which shows what can happen when parents take the trouble to study along with their children and speak the language at home."

   "In that case," Billy piped up, "I can't wait to take my next math test. My parents are both squares, and they speak in circles."

3. The boy's impatient math teacher snarled, "And just how far are you from the correct answer?"

   To which the boy replied, "Three seats, sir."

4. "Dad," said Tyrone, "I'm late for football practice. Would you please do my homework for me?"

The teen's father said irately, "Son, it just wouldn't be right."

"That's okay," replied the boy. "At least you could try."

5. Then there was the tragic case of the 6 which starved because 7-8-9.

6. Q: What's 6.9?
A: Something great, broken up by a period.

MEMORY

1. No one believes him, but Athelstane swears he has the greatest memory in history: He remembers going to a party with his father and going home with his mother.

THE MILITARY   *See* THE ALAMO

1. The Israeli soldier had been in the army only a week, but already he was sick of the long hours and regimentation. He asked his superior officer for leave. The officer laughed and said he could have a weekend pass under one condition: He had to capture a Syrian tank.

Undaunted, the soldier left and an hour later returned with a spanking new Syrian tank.

Shocked, the commanding officer walked over as the soldier climbed from the hatch.

"I don't believe it!" he said, running his hand along the bazooka plate. "You must tell me how you *did* it."

"Simple," said the soldier. "I drove into the DMZ, saw a Syrian soldier, asked him if he wanted a weekend pass, and we swapped tanks."

2. Then there was the sleek new cruiser that the navy nicknamed "Nympho" because there was no problem getting her out of her slip or filling her with seamen.

3. "I suppose," said the heartless drill instructor to the new recruit, "that when I die, you'll make a special trip to my grave just to spit on it."

"Not me, sir," said the young man. "When I get out of here I'm never standing in line again."

4. That same autocratic sergeant approached another new recruit and demanded, "What were *you* before you were drafted?"

To which the young man replied, "Happy, sir."

5. After spending a day entertaining the troops, the all-girl singing group was approached by the base commander.

"Would you girls like to mess with the enlisted men or the officers this evening?"

"It doesn't matter to us," one of the girls replied, "but first we'd like something to eat."

6. Hillbilly Herman was drafted, and on his first day as an enlisted man he was given a comb; the next day the army barber sheared off his hair. On the third day he was given a toothbrush; the next day the army dentist yanked several of his teeth. On the fifth day he was given a jockstrap; that afternoon Herman went AWOL.

7. It was an awful winter at Valley Forge, and, realizing he had to do something to keep his men from freezing, General Washington decided to quarter as many as possible in the surrounding village.

Mustering the men, he set out. The first place they reached was a tailor's shop. Though the man had a family of ten, he said he would gladly make room for one soldier.

"All right," said the grateful general, "I'll leave you with Cox. He's the shortest man in the regiment and will inconvenience you the least."

Moving on through the bitter winds, the general came to what was obviously a brothel. Although his morality was offended by the thought of staying there, he knew the welfare of his men must come first. Thus, he rapped on the door.

When the madam arrived, General Washington doffed his hat and said, "My good woman, my troops need warm beds for the night. If there is any way you could accommodate us, it would be deeply appreciated."

Worried that the men would monopolize her girls, she said dubiously, "How many are you?"

"Forty," he said, "without Cox."

The madam sighed, "In that case, come right in."

8. Inspecting the field where the new recruits were running through camouflage exercises, the general was right pleased until suddenly a man disguised as a tree started screaming and shucked off his disguise of branches and leaves.

Livid with rage, the general ordered the panicked private to come to his tent.

"Soldier," he said when the man had calmed somewhat, "do you realize that if this had been a combat situation your irresponsible behavior might have gotten your entire regiment killed?"

"I'm sorry, sir," the soldier replied, "I really am."

"Sorry isn't enough!" the general boomed. "I want to know what happened!"

"Well, sir," the soldier began, "with all due respect, I stood perfectly still when a woodpecker came along and started poking at my arm. And I didn't so much as flinch when a dog wandered over and tipped a kidney on my leg.

But, sir . . . it was the squirrels that finally got to me."

"The squirrels?"

"Yes sir. It didn't bother me when they ran up my pants leg, but I just couldn't take it when one said to the other, 'Let's eat one now and save the other for winter. . . .'"

9. It was 5:00 A.M., and, throwing open the door of the barracks, the sergeant shouted at the top of his lungs, "Fall in, you bastards . . . on the double!"

There was a mad scurrying as the men jumped into their clothing and came to order. Much to his surprise, however, Private Moss didn't budge. He just lay in his bed reading a magazine.

"Well?" the sergeant boomed.

Moss looked up. "My, there certainly are a lot of them, eh, Sarge?"

10. The soldier had been in training for six weeks before he was finally given leave.

"Darling," he wrote to his wife, "I'll be arriving at the airport on Sunday. But let me warn you: You'd better reserve a hotel room nearby."

Just before he left, the soldier received this note from his wife: "Darling," it said, "I'll be there to meet you. But let me warn you: You'd better be the first guy off the plane."

11. Then there's the historian who points out that

the German invasion of Poland in 1939 might have taken longer if the Poles had been armed with more than hand grenades. The courageous defenders threw them at the Germans, but the enemy simply caught them, pulled the pins, and hurled them back.

12. The history teacher had a policy of letting people who had been a part of history lecture his class whenever possible.

When it came time to teach the history of the First World War, he asked a Swedish neighbor of his to talk about his experience flying for the British air force.

"Vell," he said to the class, "von day I remember vell vas vhen ve vas flying our Schpads over Chermany . . . and all of a zudden zeez two Fuckers fly at us from ze sun. At vonce, I did a loop, but ze Fuckers stayed on my tail. So I did anudder, and still ze Fuckers vus wit me."

"Excuse me," the teacher interrupted, "but I think I should point out to the class that the German planes to which our guest is referring are Fokkers, which were a sturdy make of German aircraft."

"Dat's true," said the guest, "but in dis case, de two Fuckers vas flying Messerschmidts."

(from Rhoda Duchon)

13. It was the eve of battle, and the general was frightened. Thinking to shore up his courage by

reading about the great generals of the past, he picked up a book on Napoleon and learned that the great French leader wore a red uniform so his men wouldn't panic if he were wounded. Taking a leaf from Napoleon's book, the general summoned his orderly and immediately requested a brown uniform.

MILLIONAIRES   *See* CLOTHING 2, DOMESTICS 2, DRINKING 6

1. "Forgive me for asking," said the wary millionaire to her date, "but you're not the type who'd marry just for my money, are you?"

   "No," the man replied. "In fact, I wouldn't marry you for all the money in the world."

2. "I'm beginning to think," said the insecure young lass, "that the only reason you married me is because my great-aunt left me a million dollars."

   "Don't be ridiculous!" her husband shot back. "I don't care *who* left it to you."

3. Then there was the man who came into money. He married a millionaire's daughter.

4. Several weeks before Christmas, the millionaire and his wife walked into an exclusive Beverly Hills art gallery. When they were finished

making their selections, they'd bought twelve Dalis, four Van Goghs, and a dozen Turners.

"Well," said the millionaire as they were leaving, "that takes care of the Christmas cards. Now let's do the serious shopping."

MORONS *See* HILLBILLES and THE ALAMO 1, ANIMALS 6, BABIES 3, 6, 7 BASEBALL 4, BIRTH CONTROL 4, BIRTHDAYS 3, BUILDERS 2, 4, BUTCHERS 1, COWBOYS 1, CRIME 3, 9, DATING 9, 11, DIETS 2, FOOD 6, GAMBLING 1, 3, GYNECOLOGISTS 3, HONEYMOONS 6, HOSPITALS 4, HUNTERS 2, 5, INSECTS 2, JOGGING 1, 2, JUDGES 8, LAWYERS 2, MAGICIANS 1, MOTHERS-IN-LAW 2, MOTION PICTURES 7, MUSIC 2, PETS 3, PIZZA 1, POSTAL WORKERS 2, 3, PRISON 2, PROSTITUTES 11, PROTESTS 1, RAFFLES 1, SALESPEOPLE 4, SINGLES 9, SWIMMING 5, TAILORS 4, TAXIS 2, UNEMPLOYMENT 2, 6, VIRGINS 1

1. The moron noticed the student walking up and down the street, wearing a sandwich board that read "Free Big Mac!" Strolling over with a look of concern, the moron asked, "Why? What'd he do?"

2. Q: What do you call the stork that delivers a moron?
   A: A dope peddler.

3. The moron was walking down the street when, chancing to look down, he narrowly avoided planting his foot in dog droppings. Delighted with his good fortune, he scooped the feces in his hand, ran home, burst in the door, and yelled, "Pop! Look what I almost stepped in!"

4. Q: Why did the moron walk around with his fly open?
   A: In case he had to count to eleven.

5. Then there was the moron's mother, who was so proud when her son won a gold medal at the Olympics that she had it bronzed.

6. Which was worse than the moronic mother who said to her pregnant daughter, "Don't worry. Maybe it isn't yours."

7. Or the moron who wouldn't sleep with his wife because she was married.

8. When he finally did make love to her he got her pregnant; nine months later he rushed her to the pizza parlor because they advertised free deliveries.

9. Then there was the moron abortion clinic: The patients had a twelve-month wait.

10. The moron came home from his first day on

the job. His wife noticed he was looking a little peaked, and asked, "Honey, are you feeling all right?"

"Not really," he replied. "I'm nauseous from sitting backward on the train."

"Poor dear," she said. "Why didn't you ask the person sitting across from you to switch seats for a while?"

"I couldn't," he replied, "there was no one there."

11. Falling from a ten-story window, the moron lay bruised and broken on the pavement. A crowd quickly gathered and moments later a police officer pushed her way through the mob.

"What happened?" she asked the moron.

"I don't know," he replied, "I just got here myself."

12. Q: Why did the moron stop moving his bowels?
   A: He was afraid he'd forget where he put them.

13. Passing an office building late one night, the moron saw a sign that said, "Press bell for night watchman." He did so, and after several minutes he heard the watchman clomping down the stairs. The uniformed man proceeded to unlock first one gate, then another, shut down the alarm system, and finally made his way through the revolving door.

"Well," he snarled at the moron, "what do you want?"

"I just wanted to know why you can't ring it yourself."

14. The two morons wandered into the zoo late one night, and as chance would have it, they found themselves walking past the lion cage. Making a great deal of noise as they stumbled past, they woke the king of the beasts, and he let out a mighty roar.

"Lordy!" howled one moron, "let's get out of here!"

"Nuts to that," said the other. "I'm stayin' to see the movie."

15. Leon was something of a village idiot, and the kids liked nothing better than to tease him. When one of the kids got a pet monkey for his birthday, a remarkable scheme was born: Training the simian to do exactly as they said, the boys gave him a cork, told him to climb in Leon's window while he slept, and furtively slip the cork in his sphincter.

The caper was a success, and the next day, unable to move his bowels or break wind, Leon began to swell.

"Y'know," said one of the boys when they saw the bloated patsy, "it could be that you're pregnant!"

Instead of causing Leon to panic, the suggestion had just the opposite effect: He took on a warm, maternal flush, and every joke the kids played just rolled off his back.

Unwilling to lose the dunce to his imaginary pregnancy, the boys decided to end the swelling by sending the monkey back. Crawling in the window, the little chimp crept over, and, as delicately as he'd corked the anus, he now uncorked it. However, doing so allowed the built-up gas and waste to escape; the blast not only sent waves of B.M. in every direction, but actually rattled windows in the next community.

Awakened by the blast, Leon looked around the room and saw the dazed monkey at the foot of the bed. Beaming, Leon swept the animal in his arms and hugged it to him.

"You're a hairy bugger," he said, "and you look like shit, but you're mine . . . all mine!"

16. Decker wasn't the brightest guy in the world, and his coworkers were continually ribbing him at the factory. One in particular, Gus, would greet him each morning and precipitate this exchange:

"Say, Decker, you seen Ben?"

"Ben who?"

"Ben' down and kiss my ass!"

Tired of falling for the same joke day after day, Decker confided in his more worldly brother, who said, "Listen. Next time you see this guy, ask him if he's seen Eileen. He'll ask, 'Eileen who?' and you say, 'I lean over and you kiss my butt!' "

Memorizing his lines, Decker went to work early to wait for Gus. As soon as the bully arrived, Decker ran over.

"Hey Gus, you seen Eileen?"

"No," Gus answered, "she ran off with Ben."

Decker frowned. "Ben who?"

17. The absentminded Mr. Jones collared his Polish employee.

"Hey Cosnofski, I've got a great knock-knock joke for you." Mr. Jones cleared his throat and said, "Knock-knock."

"Who's there?"

Jones' features clouded. "Shit, Cosnofski, I forgot the damn joke!"

The Pole said, "Shit-Cosnofski-I-forgot-the-damn-joke-*who*?"

MOTHERS-IN-LAW

1. Q: How can you tell good mushrooms from bad ones?
   A: Serve them to your mother-in-law. If she drops dead, they're good.

2. "What do you think?" Bernie asked Bill as they

drove home from work. "I got a new TV for my mother-in-law."

"Sounds like a good swap to me," Bill observed.

3. The bigamist finally discovered something worse than being caught: having two mothers-in-law. . . .

4. Q: What's the difference between a mother-in-law and a bag of manure?
A: The bag.

5. Then there was the man who had mixed emotions when he saw his Jaguar being backed off a cliff by his mother-in-law. . . .

6. Weakened by years of sonorous gonging, the pedestal of big old grandfather clock finally fell apart, causing the clock to tumble forward. It barely missed Van's mother-in-law as it fell.

Upon learning of the near-miss, Van sighed, "That clock always *was* slow."

MOTION PICTURES   *See* MOVIE THEATERS
and EXTRATERRESTRIALS 2,
MORONS 14, SLEEP 1

1. After viewing the screen test of an aspiring actress, the producer said sadly, "Young woman,

I'm afraid that it would take an act of Congress to get you into motion pictures."

To which the young lady replied, "I'm game," and began to strip.

2. "I've finally figured out the ratings system," one usher said to the other. " 'G' means the hero gets the girl, 'R' means the villain gets the girl, and 'X' means everyone gets the girl."

3. Upon meeting her favorite movie star, Chrissie was delighted to hear that he was writing his memoirs.

"But," said the matinee idol, "they're so hot I'm having them published posthumously."

"How nice!" Chrissie replied. "I sure hope that will be soon!"

4. Then there was the ambitious starlet who made her way to the top. . . .

5. She wasn't quite so promiscuous, however, as the girl who went to Hollywood so she could make love under the stars.

6. Much to her delight, the buxom starlet discovered that Hollywood was a place where lovely frames ended up in pictures.

7. It had required nearly forty takes, but the scene was finished. The instant it was in the can, the

actor ran to the nearest phone and called his agent.

"I'm so excited!" he blurt. "The director just told me he's making two films with me!"

"Two?" said the mystified agent.

"Yes," burbled the actor, "my first and my last."

8. One day St. Peter approached Cecil B. De Mille, who was lying comfortably on a cloud.

"You know," said St. Peter, "things are getting pretty dull up here. God was thinking it would be a good idea if you make a movie."

"A movie?" squawked De Mille. "But I made so many of those when I was alive. All I want to do is rest."

"Think about it, though," urged St. Peter. "You could have a script by Shakespeare, sets designed by da Vinci, Bernhardt as your star—"

Intrigued, De Mille said, "You've got a point. Okay, I'll get to work."

St. Peter clapped his hands with delight, but his mood quickly sobered. "There is one thing, however," he said, shifting uneasily from one sandaled foot to another. "There's this girl who's a close friend of God's. . . ."

9. The producer and director were casting for a new musical when the former had the audacity to test his mistress for the part of a singer/

dancer. When she finished, the producer turned to the director.

"Her voice isn't much, but it can be dubbed. What's important is what you think of her execution."

With uncharacteristic candor the director replied, "I'm in favor."

MOVIE THEATERS   *See* MOTION PICTURES
and DOGS 9

1. Returning to her seat after visiting the necessary, the woman asked a man at the end of the row, "Pardon me, but did I step on your foot before?"

   Expecting an apology, the man said, "It so happens you did."

   The woman nodded. "Good. Then this is my row."

2. Q: What's the difference between a church and a movie theater?
   A: In church they say, "Pray in the name of Jesus." In a movie theater they say, "Shut up, for Christ's sake!"

3. Noticing a man stretched across three seats, the usher walked over. "I'm sorry, sir, but you're only allowed one seat."

The man snorted but didn't budge.

"Sir, if you don't move I'll have to get the manager."

Again the man snorted and stayed where he was.

Red with anger, the usher went and got the manager, who had no better luck convincing the fellow to move. Though he didn't want to make a scene, the manager had no choice but to get a police officer. The cop looked down at the stubborn fellow.

"Awright," he said, "what's yer name, joker?"

The man mumbled, "Joe."

"An' where ya from, Joe?"

Joe answered, "The balcony."

MURDER   *See* CRIME, DEATH
                         and JURIES 1, MARRIAGE 12

1. His philandering wife was constantly going about in the skimpiest of outfits, and Mr. Clemens had had enough. Deciding he'd like to see her in something long and flowing, he pushed her in the Mississippi River.

2. "Imagine," said Clarice's friend, "your husband drowned and left you ten million dollars. And he couldn't even read or write."

   Clarice smiled. "He couldn't swim, either."

1. Oliver arrived at the party with his new companion, a man just twelve inches high. Spotting a piano in the corner of the parlor, the companion ran right over and began playing.

   "Say, he's fantastic!" said one of Oliver's friends. "Where did you ever find him?"

   Oliver said sadly, "He was a gift from a handicapped genie."

   "Handicapped."

   Oliver nodded. "Hard of hearing. I told the bastard I wanted a foot-long *penis.*"

2. The young man was enjoying the Van Cliburn concert until his not very bright date tapped him on the shoulder.

   "What's he playing?" she whispered.

   "Chopin's Polonaise in A-flat." But the woman continued to stare, so he said, "A piano."

3. The snob insisted that anyone with half a mind could write a rock song, since that was all it took. . . .

4. The snob conceded, though, that if Caruso had worn pants that tight, he'd have screamed, too.

1. The T'malas had been unconquered for centuries, and legend had it that they would remain undefeated as long as no harm befell their solid gold throne.

   As it happened, the M'balas stormed the T'mala village one day, and the fighting was furious. The thatched huts of the defenders were put to the torch, and their fields were burned.

   While the battle raged, a group of T'malas sought to protect the throne by carrying it to the second floor of the chief's hut. Unfortunately, the straw floor gave way, and the throne crashed to the ground. It shattered, and, demoralized, the T'malas surrendered. The moral of the story: People who live in grass houses shouldn't stow thrones.

2. Aware of the danger, two mercenaries went panning for gold in the sacred river of the ancient Lawandi people. Unfortunately, the natives discovered what they were doing, and, capturing the men, brought them before the chief.

   The tribal leader was unmerciful. "For what you did," he declared, "you must pay. You must choose between death or bunjee."

The prisoners looked at each other.

"I don't know what bunjee is," said one, "but it's got to be better than death." Drawing his shoulders drawn back and holding his head very high, the mercenary said, "Sire, I choose bunjee!"

Nodding, the chief gestured and two of his warriors came over, grabbing the prisoner by either arm. Digging a deep hole and burying him to his chin in the sand, they poured honey over his head, and for a full day watched with delight as ants swarmed all around the helpless fellow. When the sun set and his punishment was ended, the mercenary was nearly insane. Dug up and released, he staggered from the village, babbling madly.

Having watched his partner suffer, the other mercenary realized he could never endure such suffering and told the chief he preferred to be put to death.

The chief motioned to his warriors, and when the mercenary was firmly in their grasp, the tribal leader smiled and said, "Death by bunjee!"

3. The African chieftain was so religious that when he ascended to power, he forebade the killing of animals.

Not long thereafter, the lion and cheetah population began to get out of hand, and, starving in the wilds, they began feeding on humans. Before long, even the antelope and zebra were so plentiful that they began nibbling on natives.

The terrified populace petitioned their leader to rescind his edict, but he refused; thus, they had no choice but to overthrow the chief. Not only was the revolt successful, it was the first time in history that a reign was called on account of game.

NEWSPAPERS   *See* CANNIBALS 8, DOCTORS 22, EXTRATERRESTRIALS 3, POLITICS 10, SPEECHMAKING 3

1. Having erroneously reported that the publisher of a rival newspaper had died, the newspaper compounded its faux pas by printing a retraction that read, "We regret that the notice of Mr. Phelps's death was in error. . . ."

2. The science reporter had been waiting for his entire career to be able to write the headline; finally NASA obliged. They sent a bunch of cows into space aboard the payload bay of the shuttle, and the next day the newspaper told all about "The Herd Shot Round the World."

3. Looking over the shoulder of the man sitting next to him on the train, the moron read: "Man Struck By Car Critical."

   "Well," muttered the moron, "you can hardly blame him. . . ."

4. Then there was the journalist who was sent to find photographer Tanaka Rhee, who had been lost in New Guinea while on assignment for *Life* magazine. After months of searching through steaming jungles and rank swampland, he finally came upon a small village where several outsiders were held in deep, murky pits.

Shining a flashlight into one pit after another, the journalist at last spotted his quarry. Jumping for joy, he sang out, "Oh, sweet Mr. Rhee of *Life*. At last I've found you!"

NUDISM

See POLICE 3

1. Upon finally getting up his courage and visiting a nudist camp, Mr. Littel was pleased to discover that the first day was the hardest.

2. On the second day, he met a girl in a nudist camp and found out that nothing looked good on her.

3. Then there was the driver who crashed into the gate of a nudist colony not because he wasn't looking where he was going. Just the opposite, in fact.

4. And a tip of the hat to the young lady who was arrested for wearing a two-piece outfit to the beach. Socks.

5. Then there was the Happy Trails Recreation Camp, which posted this sign after Labor Day: "Clothed for the Winter."

6. Which wasn't quite as unusual as the alluring summertime sign, "Please Bare With Us."

7. Q: How can you spot a nearsighted man in a nudist colony?
A: It isn't hard.

NYMPHOMANIACS   *See* SEX

1. The nymphomaniac had a terrific attitude toward sex: It was every man for herself.

2. "Nature was unkind to her," said one man to another about his latest girlfriend, "but she makes up for it."

3. Then there was the nymphomaniac who paid her shrink in advances.

4. And the sexually active lass who was hired by a health club to welcome new members.

5. As well as the nymphomaniac whose favorite breakfast was him and eggs. . . .

1. Mr. Dithers turned to his scatterbrained secretary and said, "Miss Smith, you've already been here two months. Don't you think it's time you learned to use a dictaphone?"

   "If you insist," the wide-eyed girl replied. "But I still think it's easier to punch the numbers with my finger."

2. Mr. Rupert was upset because his boss, Mr. Clark, told him to reduce his two-person division by half. That meant he had to fire either Jack or Jill, both of whom he deeply respected.

   Troubled by the prospect, he called Jill into his office and shut the door. Mr. Clark happened to be passing by just then and waited to see what would happen; a few seconds later the beautiful young woman stormed from Mr. Rupert's office, grabbed her purse, and left the building.

   Mr. Clark walked over to the dismayed Mr. Rupert.

   "I see you decided to fire Jill."

   Mr. Rupert shook his head. "No sir, I never got that far."

   "What do you mean?" asked his surprised boss.

"Well, sir, all I said was, 'Jill, I don't know whether to lay you or Jack off,' and she was gone!"

3. "Boss!" howled the astonished Mr. Biddle, "Miss Jones wore a see-through blouse to work today!"

Waving his employee away, the harried captain of industry snapped, "I'll have to look into it later."

4. Faced with hard times, the company offered a bonus of one hundred dollars to any employee who could come up with a way of saving money. The bonus went to the young woman in accounting who suggested limiting future bonuses to ten dollars.

5. Waking up with a terrible hangover after the office Christmas party, Jack turned to his wife. "Jesus, would you believe I can't remember a thing that happened last night!"

"It's just as well," replied Mary. "You got into an argument with your boss and he fired you."

"He did!" shouted Jack. "After all I've done for him, too! Well, screw the bastard!"

"I did," said Mary. "You go back to work tomorrow."

6. The young office worker had put it off long enough: Hitching up his courage, he went to his boss and demanded a raise.

The boss sat back in her seat and said, "Jim, because of your *parva leves capiunt animas* nature, and the *parturient montes, nascetur ridiculus mus* bottom line of your division, I say to you *ad calendas graecas*."

The young man was dumbfounded. "Excuse me," he said sheepishly, "but I don't get it."

The woman smiled. "That's right."

7. "You're hired!" panted the officer manager after seducing the lovely young job applicant. After a moment, however, her beauty got the best of him and he said, "Now, how about trying for a raise?"

8. Camping by the Colorado River, a woman was surprised to see a man rowing down the river screaming, "No! No! No!" Spotting another woman down the shore, she ran over.

"Say," she said quickly, "shouldn't we do something to help that man? He seems to be in distress."

The other woman looked up, her expression placid. "Oh, he's my husband, and he's just fine."

"If he's fine, then why is he rowing down the river screaming 'no'?"

The other woman smiled. "During the week he's a corporate 'yes' man."

9. The senile chairman of the board walked into

the meeting, ponderously took his seat, and looked to his left.

"My word," he muttered, "look at you, Laurence! You've lost weight, got rid of your eyeglasses, and—correct me if I'm wrong—but even the color of your hair is different."

The senior VP squirmed uneasily. "Excuse me, Mr. Eisner, but . . . I'm not Laurence."

"Good Lord!" the old man exclaimed, "you've even changed your name!"

10. Then there were the workers at the mint who went on strike to make less money.

11. The young woman stood before the judge and explained that she couldn't serve on his jury because of her job. When she was finished, he boomed, "And are you presumptuous to think the company can't do without you, Ms. Purdys?"

"Not at all," she replied sincerely, "it'll get along just fine. And if my boss finds that out, I'm dead."

12. Q: What's the difference between a hard worker and a lazy one?

A: None. Both are fired with enthusiasm.

OPTOMETRISTS   *See* DOCTORS

1. Mrs. Fenimore couldn't see the eye chart in Dr. Getty's office; she also was unable to read the numbers in the color blindness test, and her stereoscopic vision tested negatively. Finally the frustrated doctor stood before her and whipped out his dick.

   "Tell me now, Mrs. Fenimore, what you see!"

   "Land sakes," she cried, "I see a penis!"

   Closing up his fly, the optometrist triumphantly announced, "That's your problem! You're cock-eyed!"

2. Not satisfied with that diagnosis, Mrs. Fenimore went for a second opinion. Amazed at the sad shape of his patient's eyes, the eye doctor said, "Tell me, have your eyes ever been checked?"

   The sluggish woman scratched her head and answered, "No, Doctor . . . they've always been hazel."

PARADES

1. Q: What's three miles long, green, and has an IQ of ten?
   A: The St. Patrick's Day parade.

1. "I'm tired of this hand-to-mouth existence," said the wife to her spouse over dinner.

   The husband shifted uneasily in his seat. "Keep your chin up, dear. The economy is bound to improve."

   The wife looked up. "What economy? I'm tired of using my hand every time one of the kids opens their mouth!"

2. "Jimmy, you're a pig!" yelled the irate father. "You do know what a pig is, don't you?"

   "Yes sir," replied the tad. "It's a hog's son."

3. "How dare you disobey your mother!" the father yelled at his son. "Do you think you're better than I am?"

4. "Ginger!" the man screamed at his daughter, "how did your new car get in the dining room?"

   "Simple," she replied. "I made a left in the kitchen."

1. When she reached the office, Joselle told her secretary, "Boy, did we throw a big party outside last night!"

   "Really? Tell me, was that obnoxious pig neighbor of yours there?"

   "Was he? That was the big party we threw outside!"

2. "Yes," said the college freshman, "it was a great party while I lasted."

PERSONALS   *See* DISEASES 4

1. Placing a personal ad for an "exceptional lover," a woman was surprised to get a reply from a man who, apart from being a dwarf, admitted that he was also armless and legless. Deciding that this was something she had to see, the woman wrote back and invited the dwarf over.

   One day the doorbell rang and she opened the door; there on the stoop was the dwarf.

   "And you," she said dubiously, "are an exceptional lover?"

   The dwarf replied, "I rang the doorbell, didn't I?"

2. Unable to find a man who liked to sunbathe in the nude, Brigitte took out a personal ad. For his part, Sylvester didn't like the sun, but he was desperate for a woman and replied. Brigitte invited him to her home, and they spent a long day in her fenced-in yard. But by dusk Sylvester realized he'd been out a bit too long: He was burned from head to toe, especially on his penis.

Sneaking inside, Sylvester went looking for the coldest thing in the house; all he could find in the refrigerator was a carton of milk and, pouring some in a glass, he dipped his penis in.

Just then, Brigitte strolled in. Seeing Sylvester with his penis in the milk, she slapped the side of her head and marveled, "So *that's* how you load that thing!"

3. Tired of sitting at home every night, an ugly single heiress decided to take out a personal ad.

"Rich, sex-crazed, admittedly not good-looking woman wants man for quiet liaisons," she wrote, then sat by the mailbox and waited for a response.

Lo and behold, the day after the ad appeared she received an express-mail reply. Her heart thumping in her throat, she tore open the envelope. Looking on, the girl's mother asked, "So? Who's it from?"

Her expression dour, the young woman replied, "Daddy."

1. While walking her pet terrier one afternoon, little Mary bumped into little Theodore, who was out walking his Doberman.

   "Say," said Theodore as his dog stopped to scratch himself, "does your doggie have fleas?"

   "Don't be silly," she replied. "Dogs have puppies."

2. Then there was Ronald, who misunderstood what his new neighbor meant when he said that the family Doberman would eat off his hand. Now they call him Five-Fingered Ron.

3. Alfred was boasting to a friend about his home aquarium. "I take good care of it," he said, "and my fish are happy."

   The friend scowled, "Fish can't talk. How do you know they're happy?"

   Alfred replied, "Simple. They're always wagging their tails!"

4. Because her husband was frequently on the road, Mrs. Delacorte decided to get a pet for protection and company. Visiting the pet shop, her eye was immediately drawn to a colorful bird with a monstrously huge beak.

   "What's that?" she asked the owner.

"That's a Crunch Bird, ma'am."

"A Crunch Bird? Why do you call it that?"

Instead of answering, the proprietor turned to the brightly plumed creature and said, "Crunch Bird my chair."

With a squawk the bird flew from its perch and, locking its massive beak on the back of the desk chair, bit down hard. Shards of metal and leather flew in every direction.

Realizing that the animal was perfectly suited to her needs, Mrs. Delacorte bought it.

That night her husband came home and inquired about the odd-looking bird perched in their bedroom.

"That's a Crunch Bird, darling," she replied.

"Crunch Bird?" he said with disgust. "Crunch Bird, my ass!"

PIZZA   *See* FOOD, RESTAURANTS

1. After ordering a whole pie at the local pizzeria, the moron added, "And make sure you only cut it in three pieces. I could never eat six."

PLUMBERS

1. "Help!" the caller screamed at the plumber, "I've got a leak in my toilet!"

   "Why tell me?" the plumber replied. "What do you think it's there for?"

POLICE
See CRIME and DEATH 4, FLOWER CHILDREN 1, MORONS 11, MOVIE THEATERS 3, TRUCKERS 1

1. Stopped by a state trooper, the salesman complained, "Listen, officer, I've got to make a call before the store closes and—hell, I was only doing sixty. Can't you let me off with a warning?"

   The trooper shrugged. "Okay," he allowed, and kicked the salesman in the nuts.

2. Later that night the trooper pulled Mr. Schwarz over and, after inspecting his license and registration, informed the motorist that he was going to have to spend the night in prison.

   "What's the charge?" Mr. Schwarz demanded.

   "None," replied the officer. "It's all part of the service."

3. Then there was the hole cut in the fence sur-

rounding the nudist colony. The police are looking into it.

4. Mr. Ruggles was driving down the road one
summer's day when a motor cycle cop pulled
him over. Giving him a ticket for speeding, the
cop happened to notice that the back seat was
full of live penguins.

Shaking his head, the cop said, "Bad enough
that you were doing seventy five, but with those
animals packed in there like that, you can hardly
see out the back window. Unless you want another ticket, you'd better take them to the zoo."

The next day Mr. Ruggles passed by once
again, and, as on the day before, the cop clocked
him in excess of the speed limit. Pulling him
over, the officer noticed that despite his warning, the penguins were still there; not only that,
but this time they were all wearing sunglasses.

"Say," the cop said, "didn't I tell you to take
these animals to the zoo."

"Oh, I did," replied Mr. Ruggles. "And today
I'm taking them to the beach."

5. As the police officer helped the bruised young
man from the pavement, he asked, "Sir, can you
describe the man who beat you?"

"Of course," he said through several missing
teeth. "In fact, that's what I was doing when the
son of a bitch slugged me."

6. The precinct's four female officers were sick and tired of Sgt. Mulvey's chauvinism and decided to teach him a lesson. Meeting for dinner several nights later, they compared notes.

"I got him good," said Sally. "I loaded blanks in his revolver. I had to lend him bullets at the firing range, and he was a laughingstock all morning."

"I stole the key to his handcuffs," said Jane. "When we went to break up tha demonstration at the nuclear power plant, he couldn't even get them off his belt."

"I got him where it'll hurt the most," said Lois. "I opened his locker and punched pinholes in all his condoms."

Just than Janice, the fourth officer, passed out.

POLITICS   *See* PRESIDENTS and CRIME 7, EXTRATERRESTRIALS 3, INFLATION 5, PORNOGRAPHY 2, SPEECHMAKING 3, 4

1. Q: What's the difference between the White House and a porcupine?
A: Porcupines have their pricks on the outside.

2. Then there was the politician who refused to listen to his conscience. He didn't want to take advice from a total stranger.

3. A doctor, physicist, and politician were arguing about whose profession was the oldest.

"Surely mine is oldest," boasted the doctor. "When Eve was created from Adam's rib, that was a medical phenomenon."

"True," said the physicist, "but before that order came from chaos. Only a physicist could have done that."

"Excuse me," noted the politician, "but first someone had to create the chaos. . . ."

4. Trying to win over the liberals in his congregation, the right-wing preacher said at the end of his sermon, "And if an airplane went down carrying the leaders of both parties, whom do you think the good Lord will have saved?"

A small voice said from somewhere in the audience, "The country?"

5. Then there was the politician who abandoned an unpopular platform not because he saw the light, but because he felt the heat.

6. Poor little Kenneth wanted a toy he could call his own, and, dashing off a letter to God, he implored the Almighty to see His way clear to send him twenty dollars to buy one. He mailed the letter, which a well-meaning postal clerk forwarded to City Hall. There it came to the attention of the mayor, who pulled out a five-

dollar bill, wrote a nice note, and sent it off to Kenneth.

When the envelope arrived, Kenneth opened it and grew red with rage. Taking pen in hand, he wrote back to God, "Lord, thanks for the twenty dollars. Only why'd you send it through City Hall? The bastards kept seventy-five percent for taxes!"

7. Then there was the senator who berated an aide for confusing several appointments on his calendar.

"If I'd known I was hiring a horse's ass," the senator screamed, "I'd have done the job myself!"

8. The politician was sitting at his campaign headquarters when the phong rang. He listened intently, and after a moment his face brightened. When he hung up, he immediately phoned his mother to tell her the good news.

"Ma," he shouted, "the results are in. I won the election!"

"Honestly?"

The politician's smiled faded. "Aw hell, ma, why bring that up at a time like this?"

9. He was the busiest politician in Washington: He spent half his time passing laws, and the other half helping his friends get around them.

10. "Isn't it amazing," a reporter remarked to her

editor after a press conference, "how politicians never say anything yet always insist they've been misquoted?"

11. "Senator," an aide called from the next room, "there's someone on the phone who wants to know what you plan to do about the abortion bill."

   Flushing, the politician spluttered, "Er . . . tell them I'll have a check in the mail by morning."

POLLS

1. Having just graduated from college, Janet was looking forward to her first day on the job as a market researcher. However, she quit after doing her first interview. Asked whether he thought ignorance and apathy were the greatest problems facing the world today, her subject shrugged and answered, "I don't know and I don't care."

PORNOGRAPHY   *See* SEX

1. Mr. Prim, the moral watchguard, was delighted when he heard that two of the nation's biggest pornographic stars had made a family film. Sneak-

ing into a screening, he was shocked to find it was all about how to start one.

2. Making a speech against the proliferation of X-rated videocassettes, the mayoral candidate said, "I rented one of these cassettes and was shocked to find by my count five acts of oral sex, three of sodomy, a transsexual making love with a dog, and a woman accommodating five men at once. If elected, I vow that tapes such as these will no longer befoul our fair community." He concluded the fiery denunciation by asking, "Are there any questions?"

Five people shouted in unison, "Where'd you rent the tape?"

POSTAL WORKERS

1. It was his last day on the job, and the mailman had mixed emotions. On the one hand, he was glad to be retiring; on the other, he'd miss seeing the beautiful young married woman he'd fancied for the last few years.

As he approached the young woman's house for the last time, he was both shocked and delighted when she greeted him in a sheer negligee and invited him in. The mailman didn't need to be asked twice, and the beautiful young woman promptly shut the door, pulled him to the floor, and made love to him amidst the morning mail. Afterward she served him a delicious lunch.

While he was finishing his meal, the woman went to her purse and took out a ten-dollar bill, which she handed to the mailman. He looked up.

"I don't understand. Why are *you* paying *me*?"

"It was my husband's idea," she replied. "When I told him you were retiring, he said, 'Screw him, give him ten bucks.' The lunch," she added proudly, "was my idea."

2. Unable to read the name on the partially ripped label on the shipment of books, the postal carrier decided to bring it to the bookstore at 11 Main Street. Entering the shop, the civil servant said to the owner, "I have a package here, and I think it's for you."

"Who's it addressed to?" asked the bespectacled bookseller.

"That's just it," said the postal employee, "the name's obliterated."

"It isn't mine," the bookseller replied cheerfully. "My name's Thornton."

3. Her arms laden with Christmas gifts, Mrs. Douglas remembered she had forgotten to mail a card to her childhood friend Faye. Buying a card and dashing into the post office, she bought a first-class stamp.

"Excuse me," she said, her arms aching, "but must I put that on myself?"

"No ma'am," deadpanned the clerk, "it goes on the envelope."

4. Then there was the magazine that was forced out of business by a postal rate increase. Announcing the awful news to his staff, the publisher concluded bitterly, "I've licked many stamps in my day, but this is the first time the opposite has been true."

5. He'd been warned that Gerber was something of a dullard, but the postmaster decided to hire him just the same. Christmas was approaching, and, if nothing else, he'd be an extra set of hands.

His first day on the job Gerber was given the job of sorting, and, much to everyone's surprise, he separated the letters so fast that his motions were literally a blur. Pleased as punch, the postmaster apaproached him at the end of the day.

"I just want you to know," he said, "that we're all very proud of you. You're one of the fastest workers we've ever had."

"Thank you," Gerber said, "and tomorrow I'll try to do even better."

"Better?" the postmaster was astonished, "how can you possibly do better?"

Gerber replied, "Tomorrow I'm going to read the addresses."

POVERTY

See DERELICTS

1. Sad to say, the Crane family was so poor the only thing they ate was sponge cake. Mrs. Crane sponged the butter, the milk, the eggs. . . .

2. The Cranes were so poor, in fact, that when a burglar broke into their home all he got was practice.

PRAYER

1. ". . . and please," Kitty concluded her bedtime prayer, "when I wake up tomorrow, let William Shakespeare be the author of *A Tale of Two Cities*."

   Listening in, her mother said, "Kitty, why did you make such a strange request?"

   "Because," she said, "that's what I wrote on my test paper."

PREGNANCY

See BIRTH CONTROL
and CHAUVINISM 2, MORONS 6, 8,
TAXES 2

1. The doctor entered the waiting room. "I have
   some good news for you, Mrs. Douglas."
   "Pardon me," she interrupted, "but it's Miss."
   The doctor said, "I have some bad news for
   you, Miss Douglas."

2. Then there was Groucho's sister, Stretch. . . .

PREJUDICE

1. A Jew, an Indian, and a black arrived at the
   Pearly Gates at the same time.
   "St. Peter," said the Jew, "I've suffered dis-
   crimination all my life. Am I going to have to
   endure that here?"
   "Absolutely not," said St. Peter. "All you have
   to do is answer a simple question, and the love
   and glory of Heaven are yours forever. Spell
   'God.'"
   The Jew did so and was admitted to Heaven.
   The Indian stepped up.
   "All my life," he said, "I lived on a reserva-

tion and endured discrimination. Will I find that here?"

"Absolutely not," said St. Peter. "If you can spell 'God,' you will know peace and tranquility for all eternity."

The Indian did so and was admitted. The black stepped up.

"All my life, I lived in a ghetto and suffered discrimination. Will I find that here?"

"Absolutely not," said St. Peter. "Spell 'appassionato.' "

PRESIDENTS

See POLITICS and THE MILITARY 7, SPEECHMAKING 5

1. Teenager Peter Wrather was walking down the beach when he happened to see someone drowning not far from shore. Rushing into the surf, he pulled the man out; much to his surprise, the man he'd rescued was none other than Richard Nixon.

The former president sat up in the sand. When he finally managed to catch his breath, he said, "Young man . . . that was a heroic deed you did. Do you know who I am?"

"I do, sir."

"Well, then, you must also realize that I'm not without a good deal of influence. If there's anything I can ever do to repay you, all you need do is ask."

Peter thought for a moment. "You know, sir, there is one thing."

"Name it," the ex-president urged.

"I'd like to be buried in Arlington National Cemetery."

The request took Nixon by surprise. "I don't understand," he said. "From the looks of you, you're in perfect health."

"Oh, I am," answered the boy. "But when my parents find out who I just saved, they're gonna kill me."

2. Not that former President Ford is perfect, either. While vacationing recently in the Rockies, his camper broke down, and he went out to change the tire. While he was loosening the lug nuts, a rattlesnake happened by; terrified, the ex-president picked up the serpent and clubbed his lug wrench to death.

3. "Sometimes," complained the presidential aide, "I wish we had a pope instead of a president. Then we'd only have to kiss his ring."

4. Mr. and Mrs. Knopf were leaving the White House after a tour when they bumped into the president.

"Mr. President," said Mr. Knopf, "I know this is a great imposition, but—would you mind?"

"Of course not," said the commander in chief. So they handed him their camera and posed in front of the White House.

5. Flying across the country on board Air Force One, the president said to the vice-president, "You know, I've got a good mind to throw a fifty-dollar bill out the window and make someone happy."

"I have a better idea, sir," replied the VP. "Why not throw ten five-dollar bills from the window and make ten people happy."

Overhearing them, the president's press secretary contributed, "Why not toss fifty one-dollar bills out the window and make fifty people happy?"

Just then, a crew member whose union had recently agreed to a wage cut happened to walk by and suggested, "Why not jump out the window and make everybody happy?"

6. Peddling his wares in the West, the traveling salesman stopped in a bar . . . and stayed just a bit too long. Becoming rather drunk, he started decrying the state of the economy, a tirade which he concluded with a bombastic, "The president's a horse's ass!"

That was too much for one of the patrons to bear. Rising from a group of friends, the burly man walked over to the salesman and cautioned, "I'd hold my tongue, stranger, if I were you."

"Why?" burbled the salesman, "how can you guys *like* that horse's ass?"

"We don't," he replied, "but this is horse country."

7. While waiting for the presidential press conference to begin, the reporter approached a man standing alone in a corner.

"So," said the journalist, "have you heard the latest joke about the president?"

The man pinned him with a steely gaze. "Before you tell it, I must inform you that I work for the White House."

"Thanks for the warning," rejoined the reporter. "I'll tell it slowly."

8. "Mr. President," said one of his aides, "I was wondering, sir, if it might be possible for my son to work somewhere in the White House."

"Of course," replied the president. "What does he do?"

The aide threw up his hands and said, "Nothing."

"Excellent," noted the president. "We won't even have to train him."

1. "Now then," said the warden addressing the three instigators of a failed prison riot, "I would like to know two things. First: Why did you revolt? Second: How did you get out of your cell?"

    One of the three men stepped forward. "Warden, we rebelled because the food is awful."

    "I see. And the cell? What did you use to break the bars?"

    Replied the spokesman, "Toast."

2. Sitting around in their cells, three prisoners were fantasizing about who they would make love to if they could choose from any woman in the world.

    "Me?" said the first, "I'd pick Dolly Parton. What boobs!"

    "Not me," said the second. "Crystal Gayle really turns me on with all that hair."

    Looking up from a newspaper, the third man said, "If I had my choice, I'd sleep with Virginia Pippalini."

    The two others looked over. "Who?" said the first. "I never heard of her."

    "Says here she's quite a woman," he replied and held up the newspaper whose headline read "Four Men Die Laying Virginia Pipeline."

PROCTOLOGISTS   *See* DOCTORS
                                    and PSYCHIATRISTS 12

1. Dr. Daniels wasn't a great proctologist, but he was resourceful: He always used two fingers in case his patients wanted a second opinion.

PROPAGANDA

1. Looking to counter the old bromide that Japanese men were underendowed, the government placed an order with an American firm for five hundred gross of prophylactics that were fourteen inches long. However, the condom company was made of red-blooded Americans who refused to let the Japanese have the last word: They fulfilled the order but stamped "Medium" on each package.

PROSTITUTES

See SEX and ACCENTS 4, ANIMALS 3, EPILEPTICS 2, JUDGES 2, KIDS 9, LEPERS 1, 2, MAGICIANS 1, THE MILITARY 7, PSYCHIATRISTS 7, SENIOR CITIZENS 12

1. There once was a male prostitute so popular that he had to hire a secretary and a public relations director. Thereafter, whenever a woman called for him, his staff rose to the occasion.

2. Then there was the madam whose profits rose each time her assets went down. . . .

3. The old-timer at the brothel was just pulling on her sequined stockings when a novice walked in. The young girl marveled at how alluring the sequins were.

   "Yeah," said the old-timer, "every day it may be the same old thing: I put on the left leg, I put on the right." She shrugged. "But between them I make a living."

4. The man took the hooker up to her room, whereupon she asked for the agreed-upon fee of fifty dollars. After tucking the money in her pocket, the whore began to undress. "Now then," she asked, "what was it you wanted to do?"

"Spank you," said the man.

"Oh, yeah. And how much spankin' do you expect to do?" she asked, bending over his knee.

Raising his hand, he replied, "As much as it takes to get my fifty dollars back."

5. Q: What's the difference between a bowling ball and a prostitute?

A: You can eat the bowling ball, if you have to.

6. One prostitute said to the other, "Last night I had to have oral sex with the foulest-smelling man on earth."

"Oh gross!"

"No," said the other, "Jones."

7. Then there's the sign on the wall of the whorehouse: "It's a business doing pleasure with you."

8. Ricky and his sister walked into the bank and dumped bagfuls of change on the counter.

"My goodness!" said the teller, "did you two hoard all of this?"

"Uh-uh," said Ricky. "My sister whored, I only pimped."

9. Then there was the prostitute who left the brothel because she found a better-paying position.

10. And another one who, after being acquitted by the court, was loose again.

11. And still another who, none too bright, stayed at her corner all day because she heard that men were going to lay pavement and wanted to see how it was done.

12. During her lunch break a busy hooker stopped to visit a plastic surgeon and told him to make it snappy.

13. While she was gone, the hooker left a sign on the door: "Out to Lunch. Go Fuck Yourself."

14. There was a convention in town, and the call girl was as busy as could be. Sitting at the bar and confirming her dates, she said, "Hector, I'll see you around seven-ish, Randall—you can come by eight-ish, and Ray . . . drop in nine-ish." Looking around the crowded bar, the ambitious lady yelled, "Ten-ish anyone?"

15. Then there was the madam who moved her staff into a small, one-story brothel to keep down the fucking overhead. . . .

16. Unfortunately, her girls didn't like her. They went on strike and came to a grinding halt.

PROTESTS

1. The protester set the American flag afire and dropped it at the base of the Washington Monument. Wandering past, the moron said, "It'll never work."

   "What do you mean?" demanded the protester. "Passive resistance is the way change comes about in this country!"

   "I don't know about that," said the moron, "but you'll never get this sucker off the ground."

PSYCHIATRISTS   See DOCTORS and CANNIBALS 6, COLLEGE 9, DREAMS 2, FAT 3, GYNECOLOGISTS 2, MARRIAGE 6, NYMPHOMANIACS 3, SPEECHMAKING 1, 2

1. "Well, Mr. Gilbert," said the psychiatrist, "why the long face?"

   "I got fired from my job at the grocery store," he said. "The boss caught me with my organ in the meat slicer."

   Dr. Ashley swallowed hard. "My God, why did you do a thing like that?"

   Mr. Gilbert sighed, "*She* wanted it, too."

2. "You've got to help me," the young man implored. "I can't stop thinking that I'm a goat!"

His analyst asked, "And how long have you had this problem?"

The man replied, "Ever since I was a kid."

3. The distraught young woman said to her analyst, "Tell me, what would you say to a patient who thought she was a set of drapes?"

After thinking a moment, the psychiatrist said, "I'd tell her to pull herself together."

4. Later that day a wild man burst into the psychiatrist's office.

"Ya gotta help me!" he screamed, "I can't stop thinking I'm a deck of cards!"

Flushing with anger, the doctor snapped, "Wait outside! I'll deal with you later!"

5. Then there was the man who went to the psychiatrist insisting that his skin was gold. The doctor told him it was nothing serious, just a gilt complex.

6. Even worse was Mrs. Stewart, who went to her shrink and confessed she was a kleptomaniac. The doctor told her not to worry and gave her something to take.

7. The call girl confided to her roommate, "I'm afraid I'm going to have to give up analysis."

"But why? Isn't Dr. Wolper helping you?"

"A lot," the call girl agreed. "Problem is, I

just can't get used to lying down for a guy and then having him give *me* the bill."

8. The psychiatrist closed the folder and stared at his patient on the other side of the room. "Yes, Mr. Allen, I'm pleased to pronounce you one hundred percent cured."

Mr. Allen sighed. "Gee, that's just great."

"I don't understand. Aren't you happy?"

"Why should I be?" Mr. Allen shot back. "A year ago I was Genghis Khan. Now I'm nobody!"

9. The psychiatrist listened to Mr. Cage's problem, then said confidently, "You really have no need for my services. I know many men who prefer jockey shorts to boxer shorts—myself included."

"Really?" said Mr. Cage, obviously relieved. "And do you prefer them with Russian dressing or French?"

10. Then there was the analyst who told his egomaniacal patient she was suffering from I strain. . . .

11. The young man said to his shrink, "It's terrible. We've only been married four years, and already our sex life is the pits. I'm beginning to think that all my friends are right: An affair's the only answer."

Though he made it a policy never to tell his

patients what to do, the psychiatrist was not above making suggestions. "The problem," he said, "is with the sameness of your sexual activities. Instead of jeopardizing your marriage, try making love at a different time, in a different way. I think you'll find a different approach more satisfying than a different woman."

The young man agreed to try, and the next week he walked into the doctor's office with a broad smile.

"Well," he beamed, "you were absolutely right, Doc. We were having dinner and she asked me to pass the salt; as I handed her the shaker, I put my hand around hers and held it. Then I slipped my foot from my shoe and ran my toes up her leg. My wife melted, and in less than five minutes we had torn our clothes off and were on the table, making the most passionate love of our married life."

"You see?" said the doctor triumphantly. "There is a sensible solution to every problem."

The young man nodded. "There *is* one thing that bothers me, though."

"Oh—what's that?"

He frowned. "We'll never be able to go back to that Howard Johnson's again."

12. Bored with his life, the psychiatrist went back to school and became a proctologist. He's content now, dealing with odds and ends.

13. "Ya gotta help me," the patient screamed. "Yesterday I thought I was a wigwam, and today I think I'm a teepee!"

"Calm down," said the psychiatrist, "you're just too tents. . . ."

14. After several years of treatments, Mr. Benson decided his psychiatrist wasn't doing him a bit of good: He was broke now, whereas before he'd only been cracked.

QUARRELS

1. "Last night we exchanged heated words," the couple told the marriage counselor.

The counselor smiled. "You're improving! At least you're arguing instead of resorting to physical violence."

"Arguing, my ass," replied the wife. "We threw alphabet soup at each other."

2. Then there was the director who was given a black eye after arguing with the studio's most stunning actress. As the studio chief glibly noted when the Hollywood press corps called for the lowdown, "You might say he was struck by the beauty of the place."

3. Q: Why did the frustrated husband end the argument by hitting his wife with a piano stool?
A: Because he couldn't pick up the piano.

4. "I don't know how the quarrel started," the man told a coworker. "My wife was trying to hammer a nail using the back of a scrub brush, and all I said was, "Darling, you really must get something harder. Why don't you use your head?"

QUIZZES   See COLLEGE, MORONS, SCHOOL

1. Not expecting to do at all well in the economics exam, Harold was heartened by the first question: In any given year, and to the nearest ton, how much wheat did the United States export?
   Smiling confidently, Harold wrote, "1492; none."

2. Of course, it isn't only the students who are dumb. Sitting down to take a test, Jimmy remarked to the teacher that he'd gone out and bought a nickel eraser specifically for the occasion.
   "That's nice," said the teacher, "but wouldn't a rubber one be more effective?"

3. Still, young Billy took the cake for sheer stupidity. During an oral spelling exam the teacher wrote "new" on the blackboard.
   "Now," she asked Billy, "what word would we have if we placed a k in the front?"
   After a moment's reflection he blurted, "Canoe?"

RAFFLES

See FUNDRAISERS

1. Unemployed for over six months, the moron was so poor that a bunch of his friends in the Lion's Club got together to hold a raffle . . . one that was guaranteed to earn him the five-thousand dollar first prize. They gave him ticket number six, filled the hat with tickets that had only number six and, further, so he wouldn't suspect the raffle was rigged, they even let the moron himself pull the ticket from the hat.

   Reaching into the hat at the front of the meeting hall, the moron pulled out a ticket, adjusted his glasses, and with said in a loud voice, "The winning number is 6 7/8!"

RELIGION

See THE BIBLE, CLERGY

1. The nun welcomed her new fourth-grade class to the Catholic school, and, as was her custom on the first day of school, she went around asking each of the children what they'd like to be when they grew up.

   "I want to be a fire fighter!" said Barbara Emard.

   "I want to be a nurse!" replied Jason Scott.

"I want to be a prostitute!" answered Jamie Van.

The nun fainted dead on the floor, and when she came to she found the children gathered around her.

"I—I'm sorry," she floundered, "but . . . Jamie, what did you say you wanted to be?"

"A prostitute," she repeated.

Sitting up, the nun sighed, "Praise Jesus. I thought you said 'Protestant.' "

2. Q: What's the difference between circumcision and crucifixion?
A: In a crucifixion they get rid of the whole Jew.

3. Then there was the man who breezed by the Hare Krishna cultists, declaiming, "I gave in a previous lifetime."

4. Returning from having ministered to the residents of a nursing home, the nun was alarmed when her car ran out of gas. Fortunately, a passing motorist stopped to see if he could help.

"All I need is some fuel," said the sisters.

"Gas I can give you," said the motorist, "but I haven't got anything to put it in."

Remembering that she had a bedpan in the back seat, the nun ran and got it, and the motorist quickly siphoned enough from his tank to get her to the nearest gas station. After accepting the nun's assurance that she'd be fine, the motorist left and the sister ever so carefully began filling her tank.

While she was thus engaged, another motorist happened by. After seeing what the nun was doing, he told a companion, "Now that's what I call faith!"

5. Moshe was shocked when his son announced one day that he was going to convert from Judaism to Christianity. Distraught, he went to see his friend Herschel.

"Funny you should mention it," said Herschel, "but my son *too* just told me he was converting from Judaism to Christianity. Come, let's go see the rabbi and ask for advice."

Hurrying to the synagogue, they told the rabbi their problem.

"Funny you should mention it," the clergyman told the men, "but even *my* son has announced that he's converting from Judaism to Christianity. You know, I'll bet there's something going on here. We'd best talk to God."

Hastening to the sanctuary, the three men folded their hands, and the rabbi said, "Lord God, all of our sons have forsaken Judaism for Christianity. Tell us what we should do!"

There was a rumbling in the heavens and a voice echoed through the temple. "Funny you should mention it. . . ."

6. Then there's the religious TV show that lost its viewers when they discovered the producers were using canned reverence.

RESTAURANTS

See FOOD, PIZZA and ACCENTS 6, CANNIBALS 10, GHOSTS 1,

1. The waiter at the diner came over and asked his customer, "And how did you find the steak?"
   "Easy," snarled the patron. "I shoved a spoonful of potatoes to the side, and there it was!"

2. The irate diner raised his hand to catch the attention of a passing waiter.
   "Excuse me," said the man, "but how long have you been working here?"
   "About a year," replied the waiter.
   "In that case," continued the diner, "it couldn't have been you that took my order."

3. Dining at Pattie's Pie Parlor, Mr. DeMille called Pattie over.
   "Listen," he said, "this peach torte is terrible."
   "But sir," Pattie answered back, "it's our specialty! We've been serving this torte for years."
   "In that case," Mr. DeMille replied, "let me have something you cooked more recently."

4. Then there was the diner who collared the

waiter and complained that his meal wasn't fit for a pig.

"I'm so sorry," replied the waiter, "I'll go back and bring you one that is."

5. "Waiter!" shouted the furious diner, "how dare you serve me this! There's a bloody *twig* in my soup!"

"My apologies," said the waiter. "I'll inform the branch manager."

6. "Maitre d'!" shouted the angry diner, "there's a fly in my soup! What's the meaning of this?"

Bowing politely, the mustachioed gentleman said, "I couldn't say. May I recommend a good fortune-teller?"

7. The saleswoman sat down at the counter in the run-down diner. It wasn't the kind of place she'd have visited on her own, but she was on the road, and it was the only place open.

"I'll have the chicken noodle soup," she said, looking at the menu. After all, she reasoned, the soup would have to have been boiled.

The man behind the counter said, "Sorry, hon, we ain't got that today."

"What *do* you have?" she asked.

"Chicken pea," he replied.

Growing pale, the woman said, "I'll just have coffee, thanks."

8. The inexperienced waiter came over, and Mr. James said, "I want chicken smothered in gravy."

"I'm sorry," the waiter replied, "but if you want it slaughtered in so unmerciful a manner, you'll have to do it yourself."

9. Milton Rice took his business associates to an expensive French restaurant. Rather than admit he couldn't read a word of the menu, he went ahead and ordered for his guests. Although the waiter's brows arched when Mr. Rice ordered his own meal, he brought the man what he asked for: a whole pig smothered in pineapple sauce. When the tray was wheeled over, Mr. Rice was shocked, but he didn't miss a beat. Reaching into the pig's mouth, he withdrew the apple.

"It's expensive," he said to his associates, "but you know—this is the only way I like apples."

10. Then there's the chef who cooks carrots and peas in the same pot. He was shut down by the health department.

11. Then there was the southerner who ordered chitlins and admonished the waiter to "cook the shit out of 'em."

12. When NASA opened the first restaurant on the moon, one visitor complained to another,

"Y'know, this place has great food and terrific service, but there's one thing wrong with it."

"What's that?"

The visitor replied, "No atmosphere."

ROYALTY

1. When the princess finally married, she was disheartened to find that not every ruler has twelve inches.

2. Then there was the nymphomaniac princess who made every second count.

3. Which wasn't as bad as the countess who, her husband was fond of saying, reminded him of a Tampax because both were stuck up cunts.

4. King Philip wasn't happy marrying his daughter to the prince of an enemy, and to make sure that his daughter was happy, he sent a trusted agent to spy on them on their wedding night.

   The following morning the king eagerly admitted his agent when he came calling.

   "Well, my loyal servant, how did it go?"

   "Oh, marvelous, Your Grace."

   "Tell me about it," demanded the king.

   "The first thing that happened was the princess saying, 'My beloved husband, I offer you my honor,' to which the prince responded, "My dearest bride, I honor your offer.' "

The agent fell silent, and the king said, "Yes? And what else?"

"Nothing else," said the agent. "That's how it was for the rest of the night—honor, offer, honor, offer. . . ."

5. Then there was the peasant girl who became a countess when she went down for the count.

6. Then there was the wealthy young Englishman Eric Bates, who couldn't wait until he was thirteen so the servants would start referring to him as "Mister. . . ."

7. "Yes," the English lord told his guest, "everything in this castle was built the hard way. Life is not worth living without challenge! The land on which it was raised? A swamp. I had it drained and filled with rocks and timber. These beams," he gestured grandly, "came from trees cut in a woods in Spain. The stone was quarried in Africa under the very eyes of cannibals."

Just then a beautiful young woman walked over. "My daughter Bronwyn," he announced. Returning the visitor's curious stare, he confided, "Yes . . . on a horse in a raging thunderstorm."

SAILING *See* BOATS

1. The two men met at a rundown bar. "Y'know," Al said to his newfound friend Roy, "it's gotten to the point where I get drunk mostly on water."

   "Ridiculous!" quipped Roy. "That simply isn't possible."

   "It is so," returned Al, "especially when you're holed up with nothin' but men on the ship."

SALESPEOPLE *See* AUTOMOBILES 1, BIRTHDAYS 3, POLICE 1, TOYS 1

1. The neatly dressed salesman stopped a man in the street and asked, "Sir, would you like to buy a toothbrush for ten dollars?"

   Aghast, the man said, "I should say not. That's robbery!"

   The salesman seemed hurt. "Well, then, how about a homemade brownie for five cents?"

   This seemed fair, and the man handed a nickel to the salesman. Unwrapping the brownie, he took a bite; suddenly the man spit out the mouthful.

   "Say," he snarled, "this brownie tastes like shit!"

"It is," replied the salesman. "Wanna buy a toothbrush?"

2. After meeting with the boss, the head salesperson mustered the troops.

"People," she said, "I've just been informed that we're going to be having a fire sale."

"A fire sale?" spoke up one agent. "But we sell insurance."

"I said a fire sale, and I meant it," she replied hotly. "Anyone who doesn't make a sale gets fired."

3. "Excuse me," Mrs. Thomas said to the salesperson, "but I'd like to try on the dress in the window."

"I'm sorry," smiled the clerk, "but you'll have to use the dressing room like everyone else."

4. "Can I interest you in a nice pocket calculator?" said the helpful clerk.

"No thanks," replied the customer, "I know exactly how many pockets I have."

5. "Miss," said the irate customer, "you said this computer was foolproof—but for the life of me I can't figure out how to use it."

"There you are," she said, smiling smugly.

"What do you mean, 'There you are'?"

"Like I said, it's proof that you're a fool."

6. After each visit with a particularly tough client, the salesperson was heard to mutter, "I wish I had fifty like you."

Finally the client's curiosity got the best of her. "I don't mean to pry," she said, "but why do you keep saying, 'I wish I had fifty like you'?"

"Because," he replied, "I have a hundred."

7. Then there's the Avon lady who walks so slowly she only visits three houses a day. She has no choice; her lipstick.

SAMURAIS

1. The Japanese lord was in the market for a personal bodyguard and, to select the most able man, he held a contest. After several trials only three samurais remained in competition. To each man he gave a box containing a fly.

The first samurai opened his box, and no sooner had the fly left than the warrior's sharp *ashinaga* came up and sliced the insect in two. Aware that he had to do even better, the second samurai released his fly and in two swift movements cut off its wings. The fly dropped like a stone. Impressed, the lord turned to the third samurai, who calmly released his fly, made a swift movement with his sword, then casually watched as the insect flitted away.

"It appears," said the lord, "that your fly still lives."

"That is true," the samurai replied. "But, my lord, it will not be the father of any other flies."

SCHOOL *See* COLLEGE, GRAMMAR, KIDS and CANNIBALS 9, DOGS 12, ELEPHANTS 2, HOMOSEXUALS 9, KIDS 2, MATH 2, THE MILITARY 12, PRAYER 1, RELIGION 1

1. "Can anyone tell me," asked the teacher, "why the Middle Ages are often called the Dark Ages?"
   Sally raised her hand and shouted, "Because they had so many knights?"

2. "I don't want to worry you," Peter said to his teacher, "but last night my dad said that if I didn't get better grades on my next report card, someone was going to get a licking."

3. Drilling her students for a test, the history teacher asked if anyone could recite Washington's farewell address. Little TJ raised his hand and replied, "Heaven."

4. Later in the drill the history teacher asked if anyone knew where the Declaration of Indepen-

dence was signed. Little TJ once again raised his hand and replied, "At the bottom."

5. Mrs. Fenwick, the comely fourth-grade teacher, recognized the gleam in little Tad's eye, the way his gaze followed her around the room. He obviously had a crush on her, and, calling him aside after school, she gave him an opening to discuss his infatuation.

"Tad, your grades have been slipping, and I notice you've not been paying attention to your schoolwork. Is something . . . distracting you?"

Blushing slightly, the boy said in a soft voice, "Yes, Mrs. Fenwick."

"By any chance," she said compassionately, "would it be me?"

Tad nodded, and the teacher smiled warmly.

"Tad, I want you to know that I'm very flattered and, to tell you the truth, I do hope to have a husband one day . . . someone who's as bright and cute as you."

"Then why not—"

"Why not you?" she asked. "Well, Tad, the truth is I don't want a *child*."

Tad held up two fingers and crossed his heart, "In that case, I promise I'll be super careful!"

6. Having retired several months before, Mr. Boniface was bored and went looking for part-time work. Landing a job as a school bus driver and given a very short route to begin with, he was

handed a set of keys and told that his bus would be in spot number fifteen the following morning.

The next day Mr. Boniface went to the bus depot and boarded his bus—which, as it happened, was decorated with Sesame Street characters. Though he felt a tad foolish driving a bus with Big Bird on the door, Mr. Boniface knew the kids must like it and put the decorations from his mind.

The first kids he picked up were two chubby girls, both of whom happened to be named Pattie. Both carried peanut butter sandwiches and as they took huge, snorting bites, dripped jelly all over the bus. At the next stop, portly Hoss and his mother came on, the woman going on and on about how special her brilliant son was and how she hoped Mr. Boniface would drive very carefully. The last child on the route was Lester, who walked on holding a deck of cards.

As they rode toward the school, Lester suddenly broke out the cards and began playing with the other kids. However, it didn't take but a minute for Hoss to start screaming that Lester was cheating. After having honked a horn that sounded like Kermit, watched Pattie and Pattie eat like pigs, and listened to Hoss's mother babble on about her son, Mr. Boniface was in no mood for more screeching. Confiscating the cards, he sat Lester in the seat behind him and pressed on.

After a minute he happened to see Lester

remove his shoe and start picking dirt from between his toes.

"Christ!" Mr. Boniface screamed, "I've had it with all of you!"

Dumping the kids at school and rushing back to the depot, he stormed into his boss's office and threw down the keys.

"No more!" he shouted. "I just can't handle two all beef Patties, special Hoss, cheatin' Lester and his pickin' on a Sesame Street bus!"

7. The truant officer ran into Kim as the youth was walking from the circus tent.

"And have you missed school lately?" the truant officer asked ominously.

Taking a bite of cotton candy, Kim replied, "Not once."

8. Young Franklin walked in the door, a smile on his face. "Say, pop, good news. Remember you promised to pay me ten dollars if I passed the math exam?"

Mr. Grimsdyke looked up from his newspaper and nodded.

"Well," said Franklin, "I spared you the expense."

9. Little Milton walked into the house shortly before noon.

"Milton!" his mother cried, "what are you doing home from school so early?"

"I got the right answer to the question."

Beaming with pride, his mother asked, "Which question was that?"

"Who put the thumbtack on Theresa's chair?"

10. "Ma!" said seven-year-old Annette as she walked in the door, "Mr. Dunbar told us how to make babies today!"

The woman looked up from her magazine, the color draining from her face. "H-how?" she asked, tentatively.

"Well, first you drop the *y*. . . ."

11. "Say," Todd approached his teacher, "you wouldn't punish me for something I didn't do, would you?"

"Why of course not!" she replied.

"Good," he sighed, " 'cause I didn't do my book report."

12. Addressing the Catholic school class, the nun asked, "Is it wrong to have sex before you're married?"

Promiscuous Polly piped up, "Only if you're late for the ceremony."

13. Then there was the student who followed the examples of Caesar, Napoleon, and Patton and went down in history. . . .

SENIOR CITIZENS

See AGE and BIRTHDAYS 1,
CRIME 13, DEATH 1, DOCTORS 8,
FLATULENCE 2, HONEYMOONS 5, JUDGES 3,
THE OFFICE 9, TRAVEL 2

1. The young woman asked eighty-year-old-neighbor Mr. Ellis, "Do your lovers have a tough time finding you in the dark?"

   "No," he said, "it isn't hard."

2. "I don't believe it!" said the ninety-year-old to his elder brother. "Your wife says you have sex almost every day!"

   "It's true," the old man declared. "Almost Monday, almost Tuesday, almost Wednesday. . . ."

3. Q: What's the difference between an old man and a penis?
   A: When you hold a penis, the wrinkles disappear.

4. You know you're getting old when you've been with a girl all night and the only thing that comes is daylight.

5. Three old men were sitting around the nursing home chewing the fat.

   "It's terrible being old," said the first. "Each day I wake up at seven and try to pee; but even if I stand there an hour, only a trickle comes out."

"That's not so bad," said the second. "Each day I wake up at seven and try to move my bowels; but even if I sit there two hours, all I can do is break wind."

"That's nothing," contributed the third. "Each day, promptly at seven, I pee and crap with no problem at all."

The first two men look at him. "So?" they asked in unison, "what's wrong with that?"

"I don't wake up until eight," he replied.

6. The doctor was surprised to find Mr. Goldstein sitting on his bed holding up his middle finger and sticking out his tongue. He walked over to the nurse who was examining him.

"Excuse me," said the doctor, "but why is Mr. Goldstein sitting like that?"

The nurse replied, "I told him I wanted to examine his sexual organs."

7. Then there was the old man who found out the difference between old age and youth. When you're young, you feel your oats; when you're old, all you feel are your corns.

8. Old Mr. Saperstein the butcher went to confession and said, "Forgive me, Father, for I have sinned. Last night a beautiful young woman came into my shop and I . . . I couldn't control my-

self. I seduced her, and we made love for three hours."

The priest said, "I recognize your voice. You're Saperstein, and you're Jewish. Why are you telling this to me?"

"To you?" shouted Saperstein. "Father, I'm telling *everybody*!"

9. Poor Ms. Tinsdale. The vivacious twenty-year-old hated sex and married the filthy-rich eighty-year-old Mr. Porter only because he promised she would see his penis infrequently. Alas, after the wedding she discovered that was two words.

10. Ninety-year-old Mr. Morley had just married a beautiful woman who was barely twenty, and the day after the wedding his close friend Mr. Goodstone came to visit him.

"So," asked Goodstone, "how was it last night?"

Morley smiled weakly. "Fine," he replied. "I had two of my grandsons carry me upstairs after the wedding, and four of them carry me downstairs this morning."

Goodstone scratched his head. "Wait a minute. Why did it take four to bring you down?"

Morley puffed up his chest. "I fought them, old boy."

11. Then there was the old woman who still had this gleam in her eye. She kept missing with the toothbrush.

12. Boldly approaching a girl on the corner, the old man said, "How much for a night of passion?"

Sensing a sucker, the girl casually replied, "I'm two hundred dollars."

The old man's eyebrows steepled with shock. "You're putting me on!"

"In that case," said the girl, "it's twenty bucks more."

13. You know you're old, says the sage, when it takes you all night to do what you used to do all night long.

14. Then there was the old man who got up one morning feeling like a teenager. Unfortunately, he couldn't find one.

15. Which wasn't as bad as the old couple that didn't miss the good old days as much as they missed the good old nights.

16. "The problem with old age," said one man to another, "is that now that I've finally learned to make the most of my life, most of it is gone."

17. Which was similar to the plight of Ms. Rutledge. She married the aged Mr. Pincus because she figured she'd get his money without having to put out much. On their wedding night she smiled as he broke out a condom and lay it on the night table.

"Darling," she cooed, "don't you think you're being a little too cautious? After all, you *are* eighty-eight."

But Mr. Pincus only snickered and moments later his bride's mirth turned to curiosity as he took cotton balls from the drawer and proceeded to poke them into his ears and up his nostrils.

"Darling," she said, "I understand the condom . . . but what are you doing now?"

Mr. Pincus took a deep breath, like an athlete about to jump into an Olympic routine. "Honey," he said, "you might as well know now that there are two things I can't stand in this life. One is a woman's screams, and the other," he said as he snapped out the light, "is the smell of burning rubber."

SEX *See* BISEXUALS, HOMOSEXUALS, MASTURBATION, NYMPHOMANIACS, PORNOGRAPHY, PROSTITUTES, VIRGINS and AGE 2, AMERICAN REVOLUTION 1, ANIMALS 5, 8, ARTISTS 1, BANKING 1, BEER 2, THE BIBLE 5, BIRTHDAYS 2, CHAUVINISM 3, CLERGY 4, 6, 7, 14, 16, CLOTHING 1, 8, 9, COLLEGE 1, DISEASES 4, 6, DIVORCE 1, DOCTORS 4, 7, 11, DOGS 5, DREAMS 1,2 DRINKING 7, DRUGGISTS 3, DWARFS 1, 2, 4, ELEVATORS 1, ENGAGEMENTS 1, FAT 2, GENIES 1, GEOGRAPHY 2, GHETTOS 1, GOLF 1, 5, GYNECOLOGISTS, 1, HAREMS 1, HILLBILLIES 1, 2, 3, 4, HUNTERS 4, IMMIGRANTS 2, INDIANS 1, 2, JOGGING 1, JUDGES 3, KIDS 3, MATH 1, 6, MEMORY, 1, THE MILITARY, 5, 10, MOTION PICTURES 1, 2, 4, 5, THE OFFICE 5, 7, PRISON 2, PSYCHIATRISTS 1, 11, ROYALTY 2, 4, 5, SCHOOL 12, SENIOR CITIZENS 4, 8, 9, 10, 13, 14, 15, 17, SINGLES 2, SMOKING 2, SUPERSTITIONS 2, TAXIS, 1, TOYS, 1, TRAVEL 4, TWINS 1, UNEMPLOYMENT 2

1. The farmer's wife wasn't too happy, but the farmer was delighted when he learned they'd rented the spare room to a nymphomaniac. Since the rooster died, he'd been having trouble waking up in the morning; now, each day, the horny lass would rise at 5:00 A.M. and crow at the top of her lungs, "Any cock'll dooooo!"

2. Which wasn't quite as bad as the parakeet who thought he was gay because he'd kissed a cockatoo.

3. Or the woman who was so in love with her priest that she chased him around the church and grabbed him by the organ.

4. Then there was the man who died at the height of passion: He came and went at the same time.

5. King Arthur knew that Queen Guinevere was cheating on him, but he had no idea which of the knights of the Round Table was to blame. Intending to find out, Arthur fit his wife with a very special chastity belt, one which had an opening lined on either side by a razor blade.

   Several days later Arthur had all his knights line up and, one by one, asked them drop their codpiece and tasset. Lo and behold, all the knights save one were missing their private members. The sole exception was the noble Sir Lancelot.

   Embracing his trusted knight, Arthur said, "Thank you, Lancelot, my dear subject. You have no idea what your loyalty means to me."

   "It meanf a wot to me altho," replied the tongueless knight.

6. "Tits," said the sage, "are a lot like electric trains. They're meant for the children, but dad always ends up playing with them."

7. The young man was distressed when for no apparent reason he found himself impotent. Consulting a psychiatrist, he was thrilled to learn that the problem was physical rather than psychological, and that his ability to raise an erection would return if he put more wheat in his diet. Running to the bakery, he asked for ten loaves of whole wheat bread.

"Having a party?" the baker asked.

"No," said the young man, "it's all for me."

Surprised, the baker said, "But it'll get hard in a day or two."

"In that case," replied the exuberant young man, "let me have *thirty* loaves."

8. Finding his wife in bed with another man, the dismayed husband cried, "My God, Jan, what are you doing?"

Turning to her lover, the wife frowned and said, "Didn't I *tell* you he was dumb?"

9. Leslie and Linda hadn't seen each other for years. When they finally sat down to lunch Leslie was stunned at how trim and healthy Linda looked.

"My God," she said, "what do you do to stay so fit?"

"Well," answered Linda, "I've found that nothing keeps me trimmer than having affairs."

"Really!" exclaimed Leslie, looking her friend up and down. "You simply *must* tell me who does your catering!"

10. "A Jewish nymphomaniac," said the sage, "is a woman who sleeps with a man after she's had her hair done."

11. Superman was flying over the city when, as was his wont, he passed over Wonder Woman's apartment. Turning on his X-ray vision, he peeked through the roof and saw the heroine lying on her bed. She was naked, her legs apart, and was writhing in ecstasy.

Unable to contain his lust, Superman dove through the open window and in a lightning-fast maneuver stripped off his tights and boldly thrust himself between Wonder Woman's legs.

"Surprised?" he asked as he proceeded to satisfy his partner.

The heroine snickered. "Not half as surprised as the Invisible Man."

12. Then there was the pederast who took to heart the motto, "Spare the rod, spoil the child."

13. Two men met on the street, one looking healthy, the other wan.

"I say," said the fit-looking soul, "you look terrible! Aren't you getting any on the side?"

The pale fellow looked up, surprised. "Huh? I haven't had any for so long I didn't know they moved it!"

14. Tom picked up a young girl at the tennis club,

when they got to his apartment he was surprised to find her slightly kinky: She insisted that instead of using his private member, he make love to her with his big toe. Tom agreed and, a few days later, the toe began to swell and ooze. Going to the doctor, he was surprised to find that he had syphillis of the toe.

"But," said the doctor as he wrote out a prescription for penicillin, "it's not much stranger than the case I treated this morning."

"What case was that?" asked Tom.

He answered, "Would you believe a girl came in with athlete's vagina."

15. Not long after the marriage, Joshua and his father met for lunch.

"Well, son," asked Mr. Bush, "how is married life treating you?"

"Not very well, I'm afraid. It seems I married a nun."

"A nun?" his father exclaimed.

"That's right. None in the morning, none at night, none unless I *beg*."

The father nodded knowingly and patted his boy on the back. "Why don't we all get together for a nice talk tonight?"

The young man brightened. "Say, Dad, that's a great idea."

"Fine. I'll call and tell Mother Superior to set two extra plates."

16. Then there was the ladies' man whose motto was, "If I'm not in bed by midnight, I go home."

17. Q: What's the difference between a stud and a premature ejaculator?
A: One's good for seconds, the other's good for seconds.

18. Mr. Mandel returned home one night to find his wife lying naked in bed. His eyes went wide and he began to strip . . . only to stop suddenly when he saw a cigar in the ashtray beside the bed.
"All right," he demanded, "I'll kill you unless you tell me where the cigar came from!"
A muffled voice came from under the bed. "Havana."

19. Q: Why is it called sex?
A: Because that's easier to spell than "Uhhhh . . . ohhhh . . . ahhhh . . . AIEEE!"

20. Mary ambled into the house around 3:00 A.M., waking her sister.
"Hey," said Patricia as Mary undressed, "did you know there's a big red *M* on your belly?"
"Oh," she giggled, "that's dye from my date's varsity letter. He feels virile making love with his sweater on."
"What school is he from, Monroe or Monmouth?"
"Whittier," the girl replied.

21. Erik met Leroy on the street and told him the good news.

"Leroy, last night I had my first taste of pussy!"

"Yeah? How was it?"

"Frankly, I was disappointed. It tasted like shit."

Leroy shook his head. "Schmuck, you took too big a bite!"

SHEEP

1. Growing bored in the fields, the shepherd decided to bury himself in his work.

SINGLES

See DATING
and CLOTHING 6, 7, SMOKING 1

1. After going weeks without a date Marcia confided to her friend, "The truth is, I'm less concerned these days with what a man stands for than what he'll fall for."

2. Watching the girl from the corner of his eye as he poured her a drink, the young bachelor said, "Say when."

She replied, "Right after that drink."

3. Then there was the young man who was slapped because his hand was quicker than the aye.

4. Chances were good he wasn't dating the virgin who finally decided she wanted to get some experience under her belt.

5. Q: What's the difference between a fox and a pig?
A: At least a half-dozen beers.

6. Then there's the frustrated young ms. who insists that all men are like toilets: They're either taken or full of shit.

7. "I don't understand it," said the girl to her roommate. "He said I had a standing invitation to visit his apartment, and then we hardly did any at all."

8. The uncouth lad snuggled up to a girl at the bar.
"What d'you say to a little ass, baby?"
"Hi, little ass," she replied.

9. Stan and Ollie were sitting at a bar, drinking beer, when a woman came over and sat beside Stan. The woman winked seductively at him, and, feeling a tad hot under the collar, Stan turned to Ollie. "I think she likes me," he said from the side of his mouth. "What do I do next?"

Taking a sip of beer, Ollie whispered, "I've always found the direct approach works best. Show her your nuts."

Turning to the woman, Stan promptly stuck out his tongue and crossed his eyes.

10. Then there was the man who prevented a beautiful girl from being attacked at a singles' bar. He went home.

SLEEP

See ACCOUNTANTS 6, MARRIAGE 10, TAILORS 1

1. The director's wife glowered down at her husband as he began talking in his sleep.

"Maybelle," he was saying, "I'm in love with you. Let's get an apartment where my old bag of an old lady will never find us."

Waking just then, the director saw his wife staring down at him. Showing remarkable presence of mind, he mumbled as though he were still asleep, "Cut! Let'd do scene twenty-seven next."

2. Over lunch one day Mrs. Finch told Mrs. Hyde, "I just don't know what to do. My husband beats me up each day."

Mrs. Hyde tried not to show how alarmed she was. "Tessie," she said, "that's terrible!"

Mrs. Finch nodded. "I guess the best thing to do is start setting the alarm."

SMALL TOWNS

1. There are small towns and there are *small* towns; this one was so small it had a fraction for a zip code.

2. It was so small, in fact, it didn't have a godfather of crime; it had a nephew.

SMOKING   See DRUGGISTS 1

1. Sitting at the bar, the buxom young woman took out a cigarette and turned to the man sitting next to her.
   "Match?" she inquired seductively.
   The man glanced at her ample cleavage. "They sure do," he replied.

2. After making love to his girlfriend for the first time, the young man started feeling cocky: she told him that the only thing that could satisfy her now was a Camel.

SNOWMEN

1. Q: What's cold, white, and holds its side when it runs?
   A: Frosty with a hernia.

SOCCER
See BASEBALL, BOXING, FOOTBALL, GOLF, HOCKEY, WRESTLING

1. The goaltender threw a party after his team won the championship, and as a special honor asked the coach to say grace.

   Finishing up the short prayer, the team's guiding light said, ". . . we thank you, Lord, in the name of the Father, Son, and goalie host."

SOUTH OF THE BORDER

1. "In answer to your question," the new South American president told a reporter during his first U.S. visit, "our most popular sport is bullfighting."

   Shaking his head, the sportswriter muttered, "I always thought that was revolting."

   Without missing a beat, the president replied, "No, that's our second most popular pastime."

1. Asked to address a local woman's club about sex, the analyst hesitated. His wife was something of a prude, and he didn't think she'd appreciate having him discuss an intimate subject like sex in public. Finally he accepted the speaking engagement but told his wife he was going to talk about fishing.

   The day after the speech, the psychiatrist's wife happened to meet the sponsor of the talk at the local fitness center.

   "Your husband," gushed the woman, "gave an absolutely splendid speech last night."

   "I'm so glad to hear it. After all, he's so inexperienced in that area."

   "Oh come now," she blushed, "he seemed to know a great deal about the subject."

   "Maybe . . . but he's only tried it twice. The first time he threw up after eating what he'd caught, and the second time he lost his rod."

2. Then there was the psychiatrist who began and ended his speech on sex with these words: "Ladies and gentlemen, it gives me great pleasure—"

3. "Did you hear my last speech?" the presidential candidate asked the reporter.

   "I certainly hope so," the journalist replied.

4. Particularly revealing was one of the politician's campaign speeches. He concluded it by saying, "I've never done anything dishonest in my life. All I want from you is a chance!"

5. Q: What do cunnilingus and a presidential debate have in common?
A: One slip of the tongue, and someone's in deep shit. . . .

SPERM BANKS

1. Arriving for her artificial insemination, Mrs. Aldiss was surprised when the attendant locked the door behind them and began taking off his clothes.

"And just what do you think you're doing?" she demanded.

"Sorry," said the young man, "but we're all out of the bottled stuff. I've got to give you draft."

2. Q: What's the difference between a man on his deathbed and a man in a sperm bank?
A: One is a man whose time has come. . . .

1. Disconsolate because she was fat and old and unable to find a man, the poor woman decided to end it all by shooting herself in the heart. To make sure she did the job right, she called her doctor and asked exactly where her heart was: He told her it was directly beneath her left breast.

   Hanging up the phone, the woman picked up the gun and promptly shot herself in the left knee.

2. Mr. Ursini stood on the bridge, ready to jump. As he was poised on the brink of disaster, Father Callahan came to see him.

   "My son, please come down from there. Nothing is worth dying for."

   "Is that so!" challenged Mr. Ursini. "My neighbor . . . remember when he ran off with my wife?"

   "Yes," said the priest, "but that was over a year ago. You've gotten over that."

   "I know," said the man.

   "Then why are you doing this?"

   "Because," replied Mr. Ursini, "he called me this morning to say he's bringing her back."

1. The handsome, bespectacled man was having yet another beer at the bar when he noticed a young man staring off into space.

"You look pretty glum," said the bespectacled fellow. "How would you like to see some magic?"

The youth continued to stare into space.

Undaunted, the other man said, "I'll bet you didn't know that on this day, at this precise hour, anyone who jumps off the top of the Empire State Building can throw open their arms and legs when they're just inches from the ground and actually float back to the top of the building."

That got the teenager's attention, and he glanced over. "You don't expect me to believe that, do you?"

Smiling, the husky fellow said, "Why, I'll *prove* it!"

Going across the street to the skyscraper, the two went to the top of the building where the bespectacled man flung himself into the air. The youth watched him fall, and, true to his word, just as he was about to hit the street the man spread his arms and legs and began to rise.

"Wow!" said the teenger upon the stranger's return, "that's far out!" Hurling himself into space, he spread his arms and legs and promptly splattered himself on the sidewalk below.

When the other man returned to the bar, the bartender looked crossly at him. "Y'know," he said, "when you've had one too many, you can be a real prick, Superman."

SUPERSTITIONS

1. "I wonder," said Johnny, "whether it's really bad luck to have a black cat cross your path."

   "That depends," said Suzie, "whether you're a man or a mouse."

2. In the bar it was tough to tell; however, as they walked into his hotel room, he began to get suspicious.

   "Say," the man asked his lovely young companion, "just how old are you?"

   "Thirteen," she replied.

   Without a moment's hesitation he ushered her out the door. "So," the startled young girl noted on her way out, "you're superstitious, huh?"

3. While fixing his tie in the pocket mirror, Oliver dropped the glass and it shattered. "Oh no!" he complained to his wife, "now I'm going to have seven years' bad luck!"

   "Nonsense," the woman replied. "My Uncle

Oscar once broke a mirror, and *he* didn't have seven years' bad luck."

"Really?" said Oliver, encouraged.

"Really. He died that day."

SWIMMING *See* ELEPHANTS 3, NUDISM 4, PRESIDENTS 1

1. Showing off his estate to his new girlfriend, Mr. Shedd said, "Here is one of my swimming pools. I keep it filled with cold water for my friends who like to swim in cold water."

"How considerate," the lady remarked.

"And here," he came to the second pool, "is a pool I keep filled with warm water for those of my friends who like warm water."

"I'm impressed," the lady admitted.

"And finally," he said, "here is my third pool."

The woman looked down and was perplexed. "But Alfie—this one's empty."

"But of course," Mr. Shedd smiled. "Not all of my friends like to swim."

2. Sitting around the hotel pool, John said to Joe, "God, I love bathing beauties."

Joe snorted, "Lucky you! All I ever get to bathe is the dog."

3. Determined to learn to scuba dive, Mr. Cousteau

spent thousands of dollars for lessons, then spent thousands more for the finest suit, tanks, mask, and related gear that money could buy. Buying a boat and sailing to the Bahamas, he felt a surge of pride as he went down for the first time.

Photographing the coral and fish, and using his waterproof pen and pad to make notes, he was surprised to find a man swimming several dozen feet below him without a scrap of equipment.

Outraged, Mr. Cousteau flippered over and, tapping the man on the shoulder, wrote on his pad, "I spent over three thousand dollars to learn to scuba dive, and here you are in just a bathing suit! What gives?"

Taking the pad and pencil in hand, the stranger wrote hurriedly, "Asshole—I'm drowning!"

4. Young Harold wasn't the handsomest lad in the world, but neither was Burt. Yet every day when Harold went down to the beach, he came away empty-handed while Burt left with a different girl. Overcome with curiosity, Harold arrived early and waited in his car until Burt showed up. Rushing over, he said, "Y'know, every day we come down to the beach, yet while you go home with a luscious chick each day, I go home with squat. Please," he said, "you've got to tell me how you do it."

"It's easy," Burt confided. "All I did was get a

tight pair of swim trunks and before I leave home each day, I stuff 'em with a cucumber. Get it?"

Nodding, Harold thanked him and hurried to the store to buy tight trunks and a cucumber. However, after two days of strutting around the beach, Harold hadn't attracted a single girl, while Burt continued to win his quota.

Frustrated beyond words, Harold finally went over to Burt.

"The trunks are fine," Burt said, "but there *is* one thing."

"What's that?" Harold pressed.

"Tomorrow," he replied, "try putting the cucumber in front."

5. The three finalists in the Women's Olympic swim meet were all novices to international competition. But all had excelled during the early going, and after several heats the score was tied; the first match employing the breast stroke would decide the winner.

The gun sounded, and the three girls dove into the water. Mary finished first, crossing the pool in five seconds flat; Jeannie finished less than a half second later. Bringing up the rear was Nutty Nadine, who finished a full ten seconds after the others.

As she completed the lap and climbed from the pool, she spluttered, "I protest! The other girls were using their arms!"

6. Bruce walked over to the pool lifeguard. "Excuse me, but what's the best way to teach a girl to swim?"

Taking the boy aside, the lifeguard said, "The best way is to walk her into the water and, putting one arm tightly around her waist, run your hand up her arm until your hand is even with hers. Then you lightly twine her fing—"

"Excuse me," Bruce interrupted, "but it's my sister."

The lifeguard sneered. "Hell, just shove her in the deep end."

7. Finding a lovely novice to instruct, Bruce walked her around in the pool. After a while, however, she became curious and asked, "Will I *really* sink if you pull it out?"

TAILORS   *See* CLOTHING

1. When Mr. Alzedo went to the tailor's shop, he was surprised to find the haberdasher looking unusually haggard.

"Rough night?" asked the customer.

"I'll say. I lay in bed unable to stop thinking about the business, so I started counting sheep. When I got to three thousand my problems really started."

"How is that?" asked Mr. Alzedo.

"Well," the tailor replied, "I started thinking, 'Three thousand sheep would make eight thousand yards of wool. That would make over two thousand suits. Two thousand suits!' I thought. 'And where would I get all that lining. . . .' "

2. Then there was the tailor who took out an ad in the Yellow Pages that read, "I'll cut for you, I'll sew for you, I'll even dye for you."

3. Mr. Daniels had just picked up his first tailored suit and was disgusted with the results: The seams were uneven, there was too much fabric in the back, and the collar was considerably higher in the back than on the sides. But he was late for a meeting, and, having no choice, Mr. Daniels wore the suit.

As he stood waiting for a cab, an immaculately dressed stranger walked over. "Pardon me," he asked, "but who's your tailor?"

Amazed, Mr. Daniels said, "Why on earth do you want to know?"

"Because," he replied, "anyone who can fit a hunchback so well is certainly going to get *my* business."

4. Then there was the woman who gave dull-witted tailor Robertson a huge order for sweaters with the provision that they be made only from virgin wool. He spent the next week scouring the countryside, turning over the ugliest sheep he could find. . . .

5. "Say," said the irate Mr. Denson as he stormed into the tailor's shop, "I just bought this coat, and the seams burst!"

"You have nerve complaining!" shouted the tailor. "Look at how well the buttons were sewn on!"

TAXES See BABIES 5, CITY LIFE 3, POLITICS 6

1. Before an audit the IRS agent said to Mr. Brown, "I'm going to tell you what I tell everyone who sits in that chair: It's a privilege to live in this great country, and you should pay your taxes with a smile."

Mr. Brown was visibly relieve. "Thank God," he said. "I thought you were going to ask for money."

2. Called in for an audit, the young man was confronted by a surly IRS agent.

"It says here, Mr. Briggs, that you're a bachelor —yet you claim a dependent son. Surely this must be a mistake."

Looking him straight in the eye, Mr. Briggs said, "Yup, it surely was."

3. Then there was the doctor who started making house calls when his Jaguar was disallowed by the IRS.

4. And we musn't forget the sage who figured out the difference between a short form and a long form. When you use the short form, the government gets your money. When you use the long form, your accountant gets it.

TAXIDERMY

See ANIMALS

1. When her beloved rabbits Jack and Jill died, the old woman brought them to the taxidermist and asked to have them stuffed.
   "Sure," he said, "and would you also like them mounted?"
   "No," she sighed, "just holding hands."

TAXIS

See WEATHER 2

1. The young woman hailed a taxi for a ride from the airport to her office. As soon as they got on the highway, a tire blew, and the driver got out to fix it. For several minutes he struggled to remove the lug nuts on the tire.
   Late for a meeting and growing impatient, the woman got out and glowered down at the man as he struggled with the wrench. "Did you think of trying a screwdriver?"
   He sat back on his heels. "No, but we might as well. I can't do a thing with this tire."

2. Then there was the passenger who was a dollar short of the full fare and asked the driver to back up until he could afford it.

TEST-TUBE BABIES

1. The best thing about being a test-tube baby is that you have a womb with a view.

TOYS

1. "There's a problem with our new, anatomically correct male doll," sobbed the VP of sales to his boss. "You can't get it out of the box!"

TRAINS
See TRAVEL
and CROSSWORD PUZZLES 1, 2, MORONS 10,
NEWSPAPERS 3

1. The commuter approached the conductor. "This morning I accidentally left a bottle of Scotch on the train. By any chance, was it turned in to the lost and found?"

"No," he replied, "but the guy who found it was."

2. The man ran to the ticket booth at the train terminal in Philadelphia. "What's the fastest I can get to New York?"

The clerk consulted his schedule. "The train on track six goes in ten minutes."

"I'll take it," the man enthused. "That's *great* time!"

TRANSVESTITES   *See* BISEXUALS, HOMOSEXUALS

1. Q: What's a transvestite's idea of a good time?
   A: Eat, drink, and be Mary.

2. Then there was the young college transvestite who decided to spend his junior year a broad.

3. That, of course, was better than what happened to the transsexual who went to bed one day and woke up disjointed.

4. Q: Why didn't the transsexual let her doctor take blood?
   A: She'd had it with pricks.

5. Q: Why didn't the transvestite go for her flu shot?
   A: The last thing she wanted was another prick.

6. Then there was the pundit who decided that if the sport of kings was horse racing, the sport of queens had to be drag racing. . . .

TRAVEL

See AIRPLANES, TRAINS and ARCHAEOLOGY 2, DISEASES 7, DRINKING, 1, 2, FINANCE 1

1. Sidling up to the ship's captain as the liner left port, the wan Mrs. Getty asked, "Excuse me for inquiring, Captain, but as this is my first cruise, I'm wondering: Do boats this size sink often?"

   The captain turned to her and replied, "No, never more than once."

2. Feeling ill during a cross-country bus trip, Mrs. Belzer went back to the rest room only to find that it was locked. Returning to her seat, she tried to fight the nausea, but it finally got the best of her; turning to her left, she threw up all over the young man who was sleeping in the seat next to her.

   Stirring, the fellow woke and was surprised to find himself covered with vomit. Turning to him, Mrs. Belzer said, "Well—do you feel better now?"

3. Then there was the French hotel that was so exclusive room service was an unlisted number.

4. The wrinkled old crone got on the train and, exhausted, retired to her bed, which was the upper berth in a sleeper car.

Shortly after falling asleep, the woman was awakened by loud snoring from the lower berth. She tried wrapping the blankets around her head, but to no avail; finally she kicked her heels on the mattress. Moments later a man's voice came from below.

"Save your energy," he said. "I got a good look at you when you came on board."

5. Finally having scraped together enough money for a trip to the Bahamas, the college student arrived, only to learn that the hotel at which he'd wanted to stay, the St. Regis, charged two hundred dollars a day. Although that included a continental breakfast, the pool, and free golf, he simply couldn't afford that much money. Dragging his gear around town, he finally found a hotel every bit as lovely but only cost fifty dollars a day. Settling in, he decided to get in a few rounds of golf before sunset.

Bringing his clubs to the hotel course, he went to buy a three-pack of balls from the pro shop.

"That will be a hundred dollars," said the man behind the counter.

"What!" screamed the guest. "That's outrageous! They're free at the St. Regis!"

"Yes," said the clerk, "but over there, they get you by the rooms."

6. Though he had been to Italy several times, this was the first time that Mr. Tepper had seen a big gaudy clock hanging from the Leaning Tower of Pisa. Approaching a tour guide and asking why the government had done something so tacky, Mr. Tepper was informed, "Tacky or not, my friend, what good is the inclination if you don't have the time?"

7. Pausing in the airport lavatory, Shockley was surprised to find a small hole in the wall with a sign above it which read "Your Wife Away from Home."

   Since there was no one around, Shockley unzipped his pants, stuck his member in the hole, and put two quarters in the slot. At once, he experienced a terrible pain and withdrew his organ—but not soon enough: There, neatly sewed on the tip, was a button.

8. A group of Americans was touring a market in India when Mr. Beesley noticed a local man watering his elephant. Strolling over and taking the man's picture, Beesley wondered if he had time to do some exploring on his own. Having left his watch at the hotel, he said, "I wonder, sir, if you could tell me the time?"

   The Indian nodded, then reached out and

took the elephant's balls in his hand, shifting them slightly.

"It's five of one," he said after a moment.

"Good God!" gasped the American. "That's incredible. Wait here, I've got to tell the others."

Rushing back to the group and telling them what he'd seen, he brought them over to the owner of the elephant and once again asked for the time. And once again the Indian reached out, cupped the elephant's balls in his hand as though weighing them, then moved them to one side and declared, "It is seven minutes past one."

One of the group members checked her watch and said, "Incredible! He's right."

Overcome by curiosity, Beesley said to the Indian, "Listen. If we give you one hundred dollars, will you tell us how you did that?"

The Indian looked oddly at Beesley, and after a moment nodded. The American promptly took up a collection among the group and handed the hundred dollars to the Indian. He put the money in his pocket, then motioned for the Americans to kneel beside him. They did so with a murmur of excitement, and when everyone was in position the Indian once again cupped the elephant's balls in his hands. Moving them to one side, he said, "Now, do you see that clock over there . . . ?"

9. It was Mr. Mandel's first trip to Japan, and,

looking to unwind after a hard day of business dealings, he went to a local bar. There he met a beautiful young Japanese woman. Though she spoke no English and he no Japanese, each communicated their desire to the other; before too long they had left the bar and retired to his hotel room. The two shut the lights and fell into bed, where they began making love.

Immediately after they began their passionate coupling, the woman began shouting, "*Gojira . . . gojira . . .* ah, ah *gojira!*" Realizing that she must never have had anyone as virile as an American, Mr. Mandel knuckled down and worked all the harder to satisfy her.

The next day he met one of his Japanese colleagues on the golf course for a leisurely day of sport and business. On his first stroke the sharp-eyed Mr. Tsuburaya knocked a hole-in-one; trying to show how happy he was for the man, Mr. Mandel shouted exuberantly, "*Gojira! Gojira!*"

Mr. Tsuburaya's expression quickly clouded, and he looked over. "What do you mean, 'Wrong hole?' "

10. When his wife missed the plane because of business, Mr. Maggin went on ahead to Bermuda. Waiting impatiently at the hotel, he finally sent her a telegram: "Having a Wonderful Wish. Time You Were Here."

11. While touring Russia the Joneses had a very pleasant walking tour with their guide, Rudolph, until the very end of the day. It began to precipitate, and Mr. Jones said, "It *would* have to start snowing before we reach the hotel."

"Pardon," said the guide, "but that's not snow: It's rain."

Mr. Jones shook his head. "Sorry, friend, but you're wrong. It's snow."

"Rain," the Russian said confidently.

"Snow."

"Rain, Comrade."

Getting red in the face, Mr. Jones was about to yell at the guide when his wife lay a cautioning hand on his arm.

"Please," she said to Mr. Jones, "control yourself. Rudolph the Red knows rain, dear."

TRAVELING SALESPEOPLE

See PRESIDENTS 6

1. Far from home, the salesman was elated when he noticed a house with a small handwritten sign on the door that said, "Bette's Brothel." Whipping into the parking lot, he knocked on the door and was admitted by a lovely young woman.

"Hi," she said, "I'm Bette."

"Well, Bette," said the salesman, "I'm in the market for what you're selling."

Smiling pleasantly, Bette said, "It'll cost you

one hundred dollars." Eagerly pulling out his wallet, the salesman stuffed five twenty-dollar bills into Bette's hand. "Fine," she said. "Now you just wait beyond that door at the end of the corridor."

Cackling with glee, the salesman scurried down the hallway, bolted through the door, and closed it behind him, much to his surprise, he found himself back outside.

Turning in rage, he saw a handwritten sign on this door: "Thanks for coming. Hope you enjoyed being screwed by Bette."

2. Calling home, the traveling vacuum cleaner salesman complained to his wife that he'd gotten two orders that day.

"But darling," she declared, "that's wonderful!"

"Not so wonderful," he glumly corrected. "The first was 'Get out' and the second was 'Stay out.'"

TRUCKERS

1. The state trooper was driving down the highway when, much to his surprise, he saw a trucker pull over, walk to the side of his truck with a crowbar, bang several times, then continue on down the highway. Two miles down the road the trucker repeated the procedure, then did it again two miles farther.

Though the driver hadn't broken any laws, the trooper's curiosity got the best of him; he pulled the man over and asked him to explain.

"It's simple," said the driver. "My load capacity is two tons, and there are four tons' worth of canaries back there. If I don't keep half of 'em airborne, I'm sunk."

TWINS

1. "Herb," said Mr. Barris to a casual acquaintance at the health club, "I married a woman with a twin sister. And sometimes when she comes to visit, I make love to the sister instead of my wife. So I've decided to get a divorce."

"I don't understand. Surely there must be some difference between them—"

"Oh, there *is*, replied Mr. Barris. "That's why I want a divorce."

UNDERTAKERS

See DEATH and FLOWERS 3, UNIONS 1

1. With the undertaker standing beside her, the woman looked down at the body of her late husband.

"He looks peaceful," the widow sniffled, "but there *is* one thing."

"And what is that?" enquired the undertaker.

"He . . . he never much liked this blue suit. I think he'd have been much happier in grey, like the gentleman in that casket is wearing."

The undertaker looked over and nodded. "I can fix it," he said, and asked the woman to excuse him. Less than a minute later, the undertaker entered the waiting room. "Madam, everything is ready."

Surprised, the woman walked into the viewing room. Sure enough, her husband was wearing the other man's grey suit and the other man was in blue.

"How—how did you ever change them so quickly?" she asked.

"I didn't," he replied. "I simply switched the heads."

2. The night watchman at the funeral parlor was making his rounds when he noticed a corpse with a cork in its posterior. Never having seen anything like it, the watchman went over and pulled the cork out. No sooner had he done so than from inside the corpse came, "Oh, say can you see, by the dawn's early light . . ."

Plugging the hole, the watchman rushed to the telephone to call the undertaker. The mortician walked in several minutes later, exhausted and rubbing his eyes.

"What is it, Herman? Why'd you call?"

The watchman, ushered him over to the body. "Sir, you're not going to believe this," he said.

Removing the cork, Herman stood back while, once again, from inside the body came, "Oh, say can you see, by the dawn's early light . . ."

With a look of great displeasure, the mortician folded his arms and declared, "Do you mean to say you got me up at this hour to hear some asshole sing 'The Star-Spangled Banner'?"

3. Mr. Benton thought he had had the last word when he presented his ex-wife with an unusual gift for her birthday: a tombstone on which he'd had carved, "Here lies my ex-wife Sonja . . . cold as usual."

Much to his surprise, however, his wife one-upped him when, for his birthday, his former spouse presented him with a tombstone of his own on which she'd had carved, "Here lies my ex-husband Bennett . . . stiff at last."

4. Then there was the crematorium owner who sold ashes to the cannibals as Instant People.

5. The undertaker was writing his memoirs and still shuddered when he thought about the most awful night of his life.

"It was late," he wrote, "and I was called to the Hotel Hulchester, where the manager said a naked man and woman had been found dead in their room. I hurried over with a pair of body-bags, and, after the manager had given me the passkey, I went to room 777.

"Sure enough, when I entered the room I saw the bodies lying on the bed. Unfortunately, the male had died with the biggest erection I'd ever encountered, and there was no way he would fit in the bag in that condition. However, since he *was* dead, and no one would be viewing him undressed, I went over, grabbed the rigid member, and took the liberty of trying to snap it off.

"That, of course, was the first and last time I ever tried that. It was also the last time I ever confused a *1* with a *7*."

6. "Every member of my family follows the medical profession," boasted Carl.

"GPs?" asked Winston.

"No, undertakers."

7. The funeral director thought he'd seen everything until Mr. Bartholdi arrived for his brother's funeral. He had covered himself from head to toe in white fur and painted his nose black. As soon as Bartholdi sat down, the curious funeral director walked over.

"Pardon me, but I couldn't help but notice your . . . uh . . . unusual attire."

"Wha's so unusual?" Bartholdi shot back. "You-a tol' me I gonna be one-a de polar bears."

1. "I can't go on like this!" the woman bawled at her husband. "My mother sends us money, my sister buys our kids clothes, and my aunt brings us food. I'm so ashamed."

   "You should be!" replied the ne'er-do-well. "Your uncles don't give us a damn thing."

2. Then there was the moron who turned down a blow job because he didn't want to jeopardize his unemployment.

3. And the steel worker whose credit was so bad even his money wasn't accepted. . . .

4. Newly arrived in the U.S., immigrants Byron and Percy went to the urban unemployment office.

   "What line of work are you in?" the agent asked Byron.

   "I pilot," replied Byron.

   "I'm sure I can find a place for you," said the efficient woman, handing him an application to fill out. Then she turned to Percy. "And what kind of work do you do?"

   "I lumberjack," he answered.

   "Hmmm . . . I'm afraid we don't have any openings for lumberjacks."

Suddenly Byron looked up. "Hey, you must be crazy, lady."

The agent was taken aback. "Whatever are you talking about?"

"Well, if he no cut it, how you expect me to pile it?"

5. Finally, though, Byron managed to get a job interview in the meat department of a grocery store. However, the personnel director nearly fell off his chair when Byron told him he wanted a thousand dollars a week to trim the fat off beef.

"You're nuts!" screamed the director. "You have absolutely no experience."

"That's right," Byron agreed, "and job will be harder that way."

6. Then there was the moron who had trouble filling out a job application form. Where it said, "Married," she wrote "twice"; where it said, "Children," she wrote, "No, both were men."

UNIONS

1. The underetaker was furious when the two construction workers walked in with the body of a third.

"Your foreman called at two o'clock to tell me

that there had been an accident at the tower . . . yet here it is five-thirty! What took you so long?"

"Sorry," said one of the workers, "We had to wait until quittin' time to see which of the men was dead."

2. Running short of shovels on a remote road project, the foreman wired the home office for more. That afternoon he received the following telegram in return: "Have no more to send; tell men to lean on each other."

3. Investigating charges that the payrolls were padded on a city construction job, the ambitious district attorney held hearings to determine the validity of the charges.

Questioning a panel of workers, the DA demanded of the first, "And what exactly do you do, Mr. Quincy?"

Realizing that he was under oath, Mr. Quincy said sheepishly, "N-not a damn thing, sir."

Turning to the next man on the panel, the DA asked the same question.

"I don't do a thing either," replied Mr. Heckler.

Folding his arms triumphantly, the DA crowed, "Aha! Duplication!"

VENTRILOQUISTS

1. Linguini was a great ladies' man and an even greater ventriloquist, and he worked so hard at both that he talked in his sleep. Fortunately, his wife thought it was their neighbor who was doing all the cheating.

2. The down-and-out ventriloquist was playing the Ozarks and happened to crack a series of jokes about hillbillies. His dander rising, one young man in the tavern finally stood and said, "Hey, Ah'm gettin' tired of these jokes! Not all of us is dumb, y'know."

   Flustered, the ventriloquist said, "I—I'm sorry, sir. It was all in jest, not to be taken seriously."

   "Hey," snarled the hillbilly, "I ain't talkin' t'you! I'm talkin' to the smartass on yer knee!"

VIRGINS   *See* SEX

1. Ugly beyond description and convinced no man would ever want her, eighteen-year-old Sondra finally opted to swallow a pin so she could experience what it was like to feel a prick inside her.

2. Then there was the not terribly sharp virgin

who wasn't upset about losing her cherry. She figured she could always get a new one, since she still had the box it came in.

WEATHER

1. Q: Why do weather vanes have cocks on them?
A: Because if they had pussies, the wind would blow right through them.

2. Caught in a downpour, the drenched young man complained to his companion, "Jesus, is there anything worse than an afternoon when it's raining cats and dogs?"

"Yes," said the other as he glanced down the street. "An afternoon of hailing cabs."

WILLS

1. The family of the late multimillionaire sat in the lawyer's office, all of them looking askance at the beautiful young woman seated demurely in the corner of the room. Jeanette had married the dead man a few months before his death, and, even if he hadn't known it, the family had recognized her to be a gold digger.

The mood was tense as the lawyer read, "And finally, to my wife Jeanette, who I promised to remember here: Hi, Jeannie!"

WORMS

See INSECTS and FISHING 1

1. Q: What animal didn't enter Noah's ark in pairs?
   A: Worms. They came in apples.

2. Q: What's worse than a worm in an apple?
   A: Half a worm.

3. Then there were the worms who were so hungry they feasted in dead earnest. . . .

WRESTLING

1. Having had a few too many drinks one night, young and macho Marv impulsively announced to everyone in the smoke-filled bar that he was tough enough to take on any man in the room.

   As it happened, the world-famous wrestler Bulky Bernard was seated in a corner and accepted the challenge. Though Marv's friends tried to talk him out of his silly challenge, the young man's pride wouldn't let him back down.

Thus, tables were cleared from the center of the dimly lit room, bets were placed, and the two contestants stripped down to their jockey shorts.

No sooner had the bartender struck a spoon to a bottle to start the fight than Bulky Bernard had Marv pinned in a combination leg-hold bearhug. The bartender began counting to three when all of a sudden, Bulky Bernard went flying; moments later, Marv was on top of him and had won the fight.

Marv's friends were astonished, and, approaching the panting, red-faced Marv, his pal Allan asked him how he'd managed to beat the towering pro.

"Well," Marv said, "while he had me twisted up like that, I saw a pair of nuts in front of me, and, thanking God for delivering me, I bit 'em hard."

"Shit," said Allan, " "you must've bitten them damn hard to make Bernard jump like that!"

"You're not kidding," Marv replied. "And you can't *imagine* the strength you muster when you bite your own nuts."

WRITERS

1. Bumping into an old girlfriend, Jake invited her for coffee and told her that he'd given up accounting to take up writing.

"That's terrific!" she said, "I really admire a person who follows their dream. Tell me, have you sold anything?"

"Sure have," he replied. "My house, my car, all my stocks, and bonds. . . ."

2. "I don't know," the world-famous novelist said to his editor. "I just don't think my newer books are as good as my earlier works."

"Rubbish," the understanding editor replied, "your writing is the same as it ever was. It's your taste that's improved."

X-RAYS

1. The medical student was shocked when he received a failing grade in radiology. Approaching the professor, he demanded to know the reasons for the grade.

"You know the self–X-ray you took?" asked the professor.

"I do."

"A fine picture," he said, "of your lungs, stomach, and liver."

"If it's a fine picture, then why did you give me an F?"

"I had no choice," said the professor. "You didn't put your heart into it."

2. Not that the X-ray professor was perfect. Because he was dating the haughty Meryl, none of his other friends would associate with him. He was, in fact, the only man in town who saw anything in her.

3. Then there was the veterinary student who X-rayed a dog's chest by the seat of his pants.

YUPPIES

1. One psychologist asked another, "Do you know how Yuppies wean their children?"
   "Not really," admitted the other.
   Said the first: "They fire the maid."

2. "I've heard that yuppies never cry," said the sage, "they just Saab."

ZOOS   *See* ANIMALS, ELEPHANTS

1. Returning home from the class field trip, Larry said, "Ma, I got in trouble at the zoo for feeding the ostrich."
   "Why did that get you in trouble?"

"Because," replied Larry, "I fed it to the tigers."

2. Then there was the pervert who rushed to the lion's cage because he heard there was a man-eating pussy. . . .